P9-DXN-232

Antiques of the future

ANTIQUES
of the future

A guide for collectors and investors
James A. Mackay

UNIVERSE BOOKS
New York City

All dollar equivalents quoted in the text are based on the 1969 exchange rate £1 = $2.40 (unless otherwise stated). Thus 1d = 1¢.

© James A. Mackay 1970

Second printing 1971

Published in Great Britain 1970 by Studio Vista Limited
Blue Star House, Highgate Hill, London N19
and in the United States of America
by Universe Books
381 Park Avenue South, New York City, 10016

All rights reserved. No part of this publication may be reproduced, stored in a retrieval system, or transmitted, in any form or by any means, electronic, mechanical, photocopying, recording, or otherwise, without the prior permission of the publishers.

Library of Congress Catalog Card Number: 73-106796
American SBN: 87663-117-0
British SBN 289 79777 2

Set in Baskerville 11 pt (1½ pt leaded)

Printed and bound in Great Britain by
Richard Clay (The Chaucer Press), Ltd.,
Bungay, Suffolk

Contents

For My Parents

Foreword

Man is perhaps not unique in his habit of storing up objects for their own sake, but he is the only animal capable of translating his material possessions into other values—of assessing their worth in terms of hard cash. In the uncertain economic period through which much of the world has been passing for some years interest in collectable objects has increased at the expense of more traditional forms of investment. What used to be the principal motive in collecting—a need to identify with the past—has tended to yield to a need for the form of security which the possession of tangible objects brings when money itself is diminishing in worth and true meaning. Thus it is becoming less important to the collector to amass objects of great antiquity and, as the supply of antiques dries up in face of the world-wide demand, the collector must inevitably turn to more recent products.

In writing this book I have aimed to show that although an object is less than a hundred years old it can still be desirable to the collector. Indeed, even when public taste plumbed the depths in the most aesthetically barren period of the Victorian era there were still, here and there, artists and craftsmen producing items of enduring merit which deserve the attention of the collector today. Since the turn of the century conscious efforts to improve design and quality have been allied to more advanced techniques of production in every field of the applied arts, and we are now witnessing the greatest flowering in the decorative arts since the Regency. The scope for the collector who concentrates on modern items is greater than it has ever been; many products of today are undoubtedly the antiques of the future, imbued as they are with intrinsic qualities which will ensure their collectability in centuries to come.

In the compilation of this book I have been given help and advice from sources too numerous to mention individually. I must, however, pay tribute to the press offices of Christie's, Sotheby's,

Knight, Frank & Rutley and Phillips, Son & Neale who have accorded me so much assistance in the past few years and to whom I am indebted for many of the illustrations in this book. The press and public relations officers of the companies manufacturing fine glassware, pottery, porcelain and silver have been most helpful, but I feel I must pay special tribute to Mrs Moira Gibson of Royal Worcester Porcelain, whose interest in this project has been invaluable to me. My grateful thanks for their help in supplying illustrations are also due to Royal Doulton, The Worshipful Company of Goldsmiths, London, and the Steuben Glass Company, New York.

JAMES A. MACKAY, Amersham, August 1969

Introduction

According to the *Encyclopaedia Britannica* 'antique' means 'old' but also carries connotations of aesthetic, historic and financial value. Formerly the term was applied to the remains of the classical cultures of Greece and Rome, but 'gradually decorative arts, courtly, bourgeois and peasant, of all past eras came to be considered antique'.

This definition is somewhat vague, though it hints that mere age is not sufficient to make an object worthy of the appellation 'antique'. The *Oxford English Dictionary* is even more vague in its definition: 'Having existed since olden times; of a good old age, venerable, old-fashioned, antiquated such as is no longer extant; out of date, behind the times, stale; of, belonging to, or after the manner of the ancients (of Greece and Rome); of or after the manner of any ancient time; a relic of ancient art, of bygone days.'

The legal definition of an antique also varies considerably from one country to another. The United Kingdom customs and excise tariff law of 1930 specified that objects manufactured before 1830 (i.e. a hundred years old or more) would be regarded as antique and therefore exempt from payment of duty on import. The United States tariff act of 1930 exempted from duty 'Artistic antiquities, collections in illustration of the progress of the arts, objects of art of educational value or ornamental character . . . which shall have been produced prior to the year 1830'. Across the border in Canada, however, the customs tariff act of 1948 defined as antiquities 'all objects for the adornment of mankind and his dwelling and all objects of educational value and museum interest, if produced prior to 1st January 1847'.

Thus legal definitions, originally designed to cover material a century old, became fixed in such a way as to exclude anything produced after the Regency period. It has often been stated that the main reason for adhering to the year 1830 is the fact that craftsmanship deteriorated after that date, and for this reason bodies

9

such as BADA (the British Antique Dealers' Association) still cling to 1830 as the chronological criterion in defining an antique.

This inflexible ruling seemed nonsensical from a purely legal viewpoint, however, and for the purpose of the avoidance of the payment of import duty the date criterion has subsequently been modified in certain countries. The British customs and excise tariff act of 1959 laid down that duty would not be payable on the import of objects 'if manufactured or produced as a whole, and in the form as imported, more than a hundred years before the date of import'. More recently the US customs have adopted the hundred years rule and, at the time of writing, objects imported into the United States are exempt from duty if manufactured before 1869.

The divergence of opinion still exists, however, as to what constitutes an antique. For customs officers in Britain and the United States anything a century old qualifies for the name 'antique'. This, of course, has meant the draining out of Britain and Europe of a vast amount of material, and with every year that passes the net is being cast even wider. Where BADA is concerned the 1830 rule is maintained as far as possible. At the great Antique Dealers' Fairs, held annually at Grosvenor House and Chelsea Town Hall in London, the stand-holders are pledged not to exhibit for sale anything manufactured after 1830. It is a source of continual wonderment to me that the dealers at these fairs manage to produce such an abundant and varied assortment of antiques in the true sense of the word. Throughout Britain as a whole, however, the picture is vastly different.

The supply of fine-quality pieces produced before 1830 is not inexhaustible. A century ago museums were virtually non-existent; now there are any number of such institutions intent on building up their collections. Compared with the resources of the private collector, their funds seem limitless. This not only means that the amount of good antiques available to the market is drying up but it has the unfortunate effect of pushing up the market value of such material as is left. Old Master paintings, sixteenth- and seventeenth-century silver, early Meissen and Chelsea porcelain, Ravenscroft glass—these are but a few of the categories of antique now beyond the reach of all but the millionaire collector. Not only do museums tend to create a shortage of material available to the private collector but, by imaginative and intelligent use of their acquisitions, they heighten the interest of established collectors and laymen alike, thereby increasing the demand for antiques still further.

While the museums are undoubtedly playing a major role in

creating the interest in and aggravating the demand for antiques, the growing interest in the private sector would have been inevitable anyway. A higher level of general prosperity and higher standards of education—discussed in greater detail below—are but two of the factors which have made the public not only more appreciative of all that is best from times past but also given them the money to indulge their tastes. More significant, however, has been the recent tendency for more and more people to turn to the collecting of tangible objects as a form of assurance in times of economic uncertainty.

The flight of money out of traditional forms of investment, such as stocks, shares, unit trusts, real estate and building societies, into art and antiques has been nothing short of phenomenal in the past decade. Nor is this phenomenon confined to Britain; in America and in Europe countless thousands of people have been, and are, putting their money into objects ranging from Rembrandt etchings to Art Nouveau lithographs and from woven silk pictures to postage stamps, while the traditional, three-dimensional material, from porcelain, silver and glass to ethnographica and furniture, has been enjoying an unprecedented boom. This situation shows some signs of getting out of hand. The devaluation of sterling in November 1967, and the subsequent run on first the dollar and then the franc, touched off a wave of near-hysteria in the antique markets of Europe and America. In the twelve months ending in July 1968 the leading auction houses of London were able to report a fantastic increase in their turnover: Sotheby's, in conjunction with their New York subsidiary Parke-Bernet, recorded an increase of 50 per cent over the preceding season—a rise from £20m. ($48m.) to £30m. ($72m.). During the same period Christie's increased their sale room turnover from £8·5m ($20.4m.) to £11,726,000 ($28,142,400). In some areas turnover was up by as much as 100 per cent (prints and drawings), while silver sales had increased by 69 per cent.

Coupled with this astonishing increase in sales, which can only partially be explained by the 14 per cent devaluation of the pound, it is significant to note that both Christie's and Sotheby's—the very pillars of the antiques Establishment—have been seeking diversification. They have conducted highly successful sales not only of material of more recent vintage than is generally accepted as antique, but they have brought under the hammer a wide range of articles which would not have been regarded as collectable a few years ago.

The great auction houses, and their host of lesser brethren, are only encouraging a trend which is already there. In the same way, the junk shop of yesteryear has been elevated in status to the antique shop of today. As the amount of good antiques available is decreasing it may seem paradoxical that the antique shops are proliferating in every town and village of Britain at an astonishing rate. The number of *good* antique shops is not increasing, nor are the good antique shops finding it any easier to obtain quality material for their stock. The answer to this paradox is a general lowering of standards in the material stocked by most antique shops. Indeed, though I visit hundreds of antique shops throughout Britain each year, I find the range and standards of merchandise displayed depressingly poor in the great majority of cases.

There is a very real danger in the belief that mere age imbues an object with the qualities one should look for in an antique. Too often one finds nondescript rubbish marked at ridiculous prices solely on the grounds that it is old. It may sound like heresy to some people, but it is true to say that not everything produced before 1830 was either beautiful or technically satisfying. Conversely, the widely canvassed notion that fine craftsmanship died with King George IV does not stand up to critical examination.

What makes an object desirable to the collector? Beauty, craftsmanship, emotive appeal, intrinsic value, condition, rarity and age are the criteria normally applied in assessing desirability. I have not placed them in any particular order, since objects appeal to different people for different reasons, but I should like to make the plea that, if only one factor is applied in a particular case, age should be least considered. Except for age perhaps, these criteria are not confined to pre-1830 material, or even to objects a hundred years old.

Since 1830, however, it must be admitted that there have been three major factors affecting the desirability of most manufactured articles and the likelihood of their acceptance—either now or in the future—as antiques. Although the Industrial Revolution may be said to date from the middle of the eighteenth century, with the development of water and steam power, the personal element in manufacturing did not begin to die out to any appreciable extent before about 1830. Thereafter, the introduction of mechanization and the principles of mass production removed the personal element from manufacturing and generated an indifference towards craftsmanship. The monotony of the assembly line robbed the mid-Victorian craftsman of the pride in his work inherent in previous generations, and this sad state of affairs has steadily worsened over the years.

It would appear that in spite of the introduction of mechanization, a lowering in standards of workmanship was inevitable anyway. In the British ceramic industry, for example, many of the fine potteries of the eighteenth century either died out in the early years of the nineteenth or suffered from poor quality in potting, design, decoration and finish as attempts were made to cut costs and appeal to a wider market.

This lowering of standards coincided with a lowering of public taste, though whether the first led to the second or vice versa would be hard to say. Nevertheless, one cannot dismiss the entire Victorian era, for example, as a period of uniformly bad taste. Much of the opprobrium heaped on the Victorians by subsequent generations was undeserved. It is true that in furniture and art, as in the material comforts of everyday life, the Victorians showed a predilection for the massive, the ornate and the fussy; but not all was tawdry or tasteless. That the Victorians were capable of perpetrating—and apparently enjoying—objects of unbelievable hideousness is true, but at the same time there were serious attempts to improve standards, both technically and aesthetically. The much-abused Great Exhibition of 1851 did more than is often realized to encourage pride in craftsmanship and demonstrate that a thing could be beautiful as well as functional. Though much that is Victorian is hardly worth preserving, there are many things which possess enduring qualities and are worth collecting, even though they do not yet enjoy the title or dignity of antique.

Conscious efforts to improve public taste and foster pride in workmanship stand out as oases in the wilderness of materialism and mass production. In England the Arts and Crafts movement inspired by William Morris in the 1880s was an attempt to recapture something of the primeval simplicity in craftsmanship—a reaction against the pomposity and over-ornateness of Victorian taste. It was a precursor of that curious phenomenon at the end of the century known as Art Nouveau (and many other names) whose ethereal shapes and sinuous lines gave way, in turn, to the angles and straight lines of the 1920s when Art Deco was supreme. These styles and fashions seemed ludicrous to many people at the time and seem strange to many others today; nevertheless, they were the outward expression of a minority in art, in architecture, in furniture, textile and ceramic design who strove for improvements (as they saw it) in the production and appearance of objects—not only those intended purely for decorative purposes but objects used in every phase and aspect of life.

The products of the Arts and Crafts movement, of Art Nouveau and Art Deco were despised and neglected in succession, and it is only now, after a decent lapse of time, that we can see them in proper perspective and appreciate that they have a great deal to offer to the collector. None of this material is in any sense antique, yet it is being avidly collected as representing the best of the period 1870–1930, and undoubtedly the furniture, glassware, porcelain and silver produced in these distinctive styles may be regarded as the antiques of the future.

In general, however, the century after 1830 was a barren one as far as the production of fine-quality material was concerned. This sorry state of affairs may be attributed to the law of supply and demand, in so far as increasing prosperity and a gradual rise in the national income stimulated the demand for material possessions, but the public lacked the standards of education necessary for an appreciation of what was tasteful and worthwhile. It would be no exaggeration to state that fully thirty years elapsed before the educational reforms of 1870 had any appreciable effect on the great mass of the British population and a further thirty years passed before a generation grew up which had both the means and the sensitivity sufficiently developed to recognize quality when it was present. Education itself has undergone subtle changes since the Second World War, and it is really only within the past decade that art appreciation and visits to museums and galleries have become a regular part of the average English school curriculum.

Since 1930 there have been several developments which have had an important bearing on the world of art and antiques. In Britain steady growth in the national income (even allowing for the rising cost of living and three devaluations of sterling), coupled with progressively shorter working hours, has stimulated interest in collecting. More and more people now have the time and the money to indulge in what was formerly the preserve of a privileged few. Formerly, also, taste and discernment in collecting might have been confined to the upper classes, who had the background and education necessary for a proper understanding of the finer things of life. Nowadays, however, not only is there a conscious effort to teach aesthetics in schools (though I doubt how successful this could ever be) but radio, television and the cinema have contributed in no small measure towards the public's greater awareness of beautiful things worth studying and collecting.

A greater general awareness of what is beautiful and worthwhile inevitably tends to encourage better craftsmanship. If the years between the two World Wars marked the nadir in fine design and workmanship they also marked the emergence of a group of people such as W.B. Honey, Mrs MacDermott, Harry Trethowan and Howard Robertson who were very active in promoting design consciousness in England. Out of their efforts in the thirties and

14

forties came the Government-sponsored Design Centre and the Council of Industrial Design, whose interests range over the whole gamut of 'useful' articles, from household appliances to postage stamps. It is now being proved that beauty and utilitarianism need not be incompatible.

The efforts of the Council of Industrial Design have come at an opportune moment, since there are so many more avenues open to the designer of genius today than there were in the eighteenth century. Where, for example, are the Hepplewhites and Chippendales of today? Probably designing aircraft or foundation garments. The amount of talent is as plentiful today as it was in 1830 or earlier, but there are far more outlets for it. Moreover, the exigencies of modern life have robbed the mundane of its aesthetic qualities. Few examples survive today of the Art Nouveau ironwork which used to decorate suburban railway carriages, or the ornamental terracotta and majolica tiles which embellished the public lavatories of Edwardian times. Probably the most dramatic example of the mundane imbued with artistic pretensions was the pictorial pot lid of mid-Victorian times. These pot lids, with their attractive transfer-printed pictures, were designed to cover jars of hair cream or fish paste, and, regarded as an art form in their own right, have long been highly prized by collectors. Some pictorial pot lids fetch over three figures today—yet at one time they were incidental to the packaging of consumer goods. Packaging nowadays is designed primarily for ease of disposal when the contents are exhausted, and I doubt whether any of it would appeal to the collectors of the future.

Perhaps it is a reaction against the tawdriness and built-in obsolescence of so many of our material possessions today which makes us appreciate craftsmanship and true worth all the more when we find it.

More money, more leisure, higher standards of education and a greater consciousness of what is aesthetically satisfying in a world which, paradoxically, has had to abandon aesthetics to a large degree, have all combined to explain the present boom in collecting.

There was a time when objects were collected for their own sakes—as examples of exquisite craftsmanship, beauty or rarity. Perhaps the reason for collecting was nothing more than the charm of owning something of great age. At any rate, intrinsic worth was seldom of primary consideration. Nowadays, however, there is a growing tendency for the collector to be aware of values and to prize his possessions not only for their aesthetic qualities but also as investments.

15

Gone are the days of the great gentleman-collectors, such as Sloane, Cotton, Harley and Hunter, whose interests covered every collectable medium and whose tastes were equally developed for paintings and incunabula as for coins and illuminated manuscripts. Even the oil billionaires of Texas could scarcely emulate today the feat of the late Andrew Mellon, who once purchased thirty-three paintings from the Hermitage for $19 million. But while there are very few private individuals who could now afford to buy a Leonardo or a Rembrandt, there are millions of people throughout the world who have the leisure to specialize in some chosen field, and the surplus cash to acquire the material for their collections. There are very many collectors in Britain and the United States, for example, who can boast of a reasonable assemblage of porcelain, silver, prints or glass, while the number of stamp-collectors in Britain alone is thought to have doubled within the past few years.

In these times of 'Freeze' and 'Squeeze' in Britain it may seem strange to speak of people putting surplus cash into collections of one sort or another, but the fact remains that there has been something of a boom in art and antiques, and there is no sign, as yet, that it is coming to an end. The auction season of 1968–9 was a record one on all fronts, with previous price records broken in every sector of the vast field of art and antiques. The amount of money flowing through the sale rooms has never been equalled before.

This is explained partly by the instinctive desire to keep assets fluid during periods of economic uncertainty and to purchase objects with a *real* value as a hedge against inflation. More specifically, the British Finance Act of 1965 has had the effect of diverting money away from traditional forms of investment and directing it into the art and antique market, where capital gains tax is *not* payable on profits from transactions below £1000 ($2400). This has attracted a great many investors in the medium range who have been purchasing items around the £200–£500 mark ($480–$1200), safe in the knowledge that, were they to sell them in two or three years' time, they could reasonably hope for a profit (in some cases of as much as 100 per cent) without having to pay 30 per cent of it to the Exchequer.

This has had a noticeable effect on the orthodox antique market, the prices in which have doubled or trebled since 1965 as a general rule, though in some cases the increase has been tenfold. Better-quality pieces have also been subject to museum purchase, not so much in Britain as in America, and there has been an alarming drain of good material across the Atlantic to appease the apparently insatiable demand of American collectors. The disappearance of top-quality items, either into museums or overseas, has resulted in the promotion of many antiques of secondary quality or importance to the first rank, and these, in turn, are now disappearing in the same way. Even damaged or imperfect objects, or those whose workmanship is definitely not of the best, are largely sought out simply because of their age. Whether this mania will continue is a matter for conjecture. I believe that the only enduring quality is quality itself, and that the criterion of age is of relative insignificance.

For this reason I feel that it is better to invest £500 ($1200) in current models of Dorothy Doughty birds than a similar sum in five antiques at £100 ($240). For £100 one would either get a greatly overpriced piece of junk (such as will be found in many of Britain's antique shops today) or, from the better class of London antique dealer, an item which not so long ago could be regarded as run-of-the-mill. In either case one is paying a vast premium for age, but it remains to be seen whether, in terms of fine craftsmanship, one is really getting value for money.

As the market in antiques has hardened in recent years, increasing interest has been shown in the products of the Victorian era, many of which are still—but only just—underpriced. As the market for Victoriana hardens attention is being focused increasingly on the Edwardian era and even the once-despised twenties. The successive chapters in this book examine each of these periods covering the time-span approximately from 1830 to 1930, and some attempt is made to examine their products and point out which possess those enduring qualities which mark them out as antiques of the future. In the same way the modern period of the past four decades is examined in greater detail, according to categories, such as porcelain, silver, glass and furniture, together with material which is essentially twentieth century in character but which has already begun to attract the serious attention of collectors.

There are hundreds of fields open to the collector who is also an investor. Some are likely to be more lucrative than others, depending on the strength of the market and the size of the collector's purse. But there is any amount of pleasure, and no little profit, to be had from collecting—provided that a sense of proportion is retained and collecting does not become an obsession.

Although specific references in this chapter have related to the English market in collecting, the same conditions apply in Western Europe and North America. If I have concentrated on the trends shown by the great London auction houses, such as Sotheby's and

Christie's it is significant to note that these companies are competing against each other internationally; the position of London as the centre of the world market in fine and applied arts is in no way diminished by the development of auctioneering in America, Europe and Asia by these firms in recent years. In the United States, however, the old-style country auctions of house contents are giving way to auctions conducted in country areas by city firms. Such auctions may have the appearance of being genuine, and they attract large numbers of bidders, not only from the surrounding district but from the cities, but the goods being sold are not always genuine house contents, and such sales are often no more than a means of shifting 'dead' stock and junk lots. Auctioneering—and antique dealing generally—have not yet attained in America the level of sophistication found in Britain or Western Europe.

While there appears no end to the steady drain of collectable material for the 'popular' market from Britain to America, since the first GIs came to England in 1942, there are indications that American collectors are now turning to the indigenous products of yesteryear. Perhaps they are not aesthetically appealing, but the manufactured articles dating from the beginning of America's great industrial revolution after the Civil War are now rising rapidly in value. Even the most mundane objects from the latter years of the last century are now beginning to command good prices, and the scope for the collector of Americana, as outlined in the next chapter, is truly immense.

1 Victoriana

It should be regarded as a compliment to Britain that the second half of the nineteenth century is universally known as the Victorian Era. Even in the United States it is common to refer to the material vestiges of this period as Victoriana, although they may have had no connection whatsoever with the British Empire. The influence of Victorian Britain was all-pervasive: Clyde-built steamers were to be found not only on the seven seas but on almost every lake and river of navigable depth—a far cry from the present day, when Japan produces ten times the shipping tonnage of the British shipyards. Britain had become highly industrialized in the generation following the Napoleonic Wars. The far-flung empire, which reached its zenith in Victoria's reign, provided the raw materials for the multifarious industries of Britain, not to mention the expanding consumer market for the manufactures of the country. Industrially and technologically Britain led the world. The Industrial Revolution hit Britain in the 1760s—a century before Germany and Italy had found their national identity, a century before the United States resolved (only partially as it has turned out) the social and economic problems which threatened the Union, a century before Japan emerged from Oriental obscurity. Britain had a head start of a hundred years on her competitors. Such rivalry as there was, in industry, commerce and colonial expansion, was with the old enemy France; but the two countries exerted a considerable influence on each other, to their mutual benefit. British influence on the empire of Napoleon III has probably been underrated; it was certainly considerable in taste and fashion from the mid-1850s onwards, and increased rather than diminished during the reign of Victoria's successor, Edward VII.

The rapid industrialization of Britain, from 1830 onwards in particular, raised the general level of prosperity immeasurably. Higher wages induced the working classes to marry earlier; the

19

effects of improved sanitation, better housing and vaccination were reflected in a sharp fall in infant mortality and a dramatic increase in the birth rate. People's expectation of life was greatly extended, contraception was virtually non-existent. It is hardly surprising, therefore, that the population of the United Kingdom rose dramatically in this period. At the beginning of the nineteenth century the population of England and Wales was little more than eight millions. When Victoria ascended the throne in 1837 it had risen to fourteen millions. At the time of her death in 1901 it stood at about 32,500,000. A similar pattern appeared in Scotland; only in Ireland, hit by agrarian troubles and the devastating potato famine of the 1840s, did the population show a decline.

The sheer bulk of population alone created a tremendous demand for what would nowadays be termed 'service industries', that is to say, for services which are non-productive in the material sense. The growth of capital and the cumulative national income also had a marked effect on the production of luxury goods. Although popular banking, in the form of the Post Office Savings movement, was in existence by the 1860s, a large proportion of the populace lived from day to day, or week to week, spending their money as they got it, and 'popular saving' did not catch on to any appreciable extent until the First World War.

Instead of putting their money in banks, people in the lower income groups invested in material possessions—then as now—by which their status in society could be measured. This intense love of material things is often seen as a characteristic of the Victorians: it manifested itself in the clutter of objects with which they filled their houses to overflowing, and in the massive ornateness and fussiness of these objects. Pride in themselves and in their possessions inspired the Victorians to instil their idea of art and good taste into the most mundane objects. For years the flower-encrusted chamber-pot epitomized the derision in which the Victorian era was held by its successors—the lavatorial joke *par excellence*. Now, however, these boudoir ornaments are avidly collected for their own sakes or to meet the demand for bizarre containers created by the current vogue in England for indoor gardens and house plants. I remember, about ten years ago, coming across a whole yard full of these floral chamber-pots in the old Treasure Trove in Birmingham (probably the biggest and best-known junk-shop in Britain at that time). In serried ranks, decorated in the styles of Meissen and Sèvres or the exotic Imari of the Far East they were an unnerving sight, but the majority were priced at under five shillings (60¢). Today their starting price would be as many pounds, while good examples of that curiosity of folk art, the two-handled bridal chamber-pot, with appropriate doggerel outside and a realistic earthenware frog within, have vanished from the market, making fleeting appearances in the better-class sale rooms at correspondingly high prices.

The present craze for floral art and the use of plants in interior decoration has promoted many other items of Victoriana from the scrapyard to the fashionable drawing room. Bath-tubs come in many weird and wonderful shapes, from the full-length tub to the sitz bath, and usually they have a wealth of decoration on the rim, outer sides and feet. Cleaned up and refurbished with a fresh coat of paint they are being eagerly snapped up as plant troughs for the sun-wing and patio. Brass and copper pots, pans and kettles are to be found in a great variety of shapes. While ornament on these utensils was invariably kept to a minimum, they take a beautiful polish and make most attractive flower and plant holders for indoor use.

The utilization of Victorian domestic wares for modern interior and exterior decoration seems boundless, given the imagination and ingenuity of today's interior decorators. It is amazing how a coat of white paint can transform a rusty iron washstand frame of the 1890s into an attractive and decorative object capable of many uses in the modern home.

On the subject of washstands it must be mentioned that these articles, once the indispensable adjunct of every middle-class bedroom before wash-hand basins were invented, are not so common as they were ten years ago. In 1945 my parents bought a large mid-Victorian house which contained several washstands, the relics of a former occupancy. Vandalistically we smashed the marble tops and used the pieces for ornamental paving in the garden. How many more of these marble tops went the same way I shudder to think, but twenty-five years ago who could have envisaged the use which would be found for these heavy and unlovely objects? Nowadays they are being cut, reground and converted into coffee tables.

Apart from their obvious uses as flower and plant holders, Victorian domestic metalware items can be converted and utilized in other ways. Small brass or copper tea urns can be wired for electric light and converted into attractive and unusual table lamps, while meat covers can be cut in half and made into bowls for wall lights—in this form they look most effective on timbered or rough stone walls. Many smaller brass or copper kitchen utensils and gadgets can provide a nice contrast and lend superb decorative effect to the most modern of kitchens; a brightly polished brass meat-jack or a row of brass ladles and skimmers most effectively balance the somewhat antiseptic appearance of today's unit-furnished kitchens. The large brass scales, complete with weights, which were used by grocers in the days—not so long ago —before pre-packaging of goods was fashionable, are now in great demand, not for practical purposes but purely for decoration. Examples of these grocers' scales were being manufactured up to about a generation ago, so they are not all Victorian by any means. Yet they represent a method of trading which remained unaltered for centuries and which has now vanished for ever, so they deserve to be classed with Victoriana as relics of a bygone age.

In the realm of copper and brass the range of collectable objects is almost boundless. There are brass and copper items connected with the hearth—fenders, andirons, trivets, coal-scuttles, fire-dogs and poker sets. To a varying degree such articles still have their uses, though few of them are being manufactured in this age when central heating is so prevalent. Perhaps it is a measure of nostalgia for the days of the old open coal fire which impels people to collect items associated with it. Whatever the reason, these articles are certainly very popular at the moment.

Copper warming-pans, which, filled with red-hot coals, were once used to heat beds, have long been regarded as suitable wall decoration. As we move into the era of the electric blanket, how-ever, the old-fashioned hot-water bottle is being promoted from the bedroom to the lounge as a decorative object. Not the rubber variety, which is still widely used, but the old-style circular bottle made of copper bound and capped in brass. This type, with a matching knitted woollen cover to make it cosy, was in use until the Second World War. Now it has been elevated to the status of 'antique' by a generation which has grown up without its bene-ficial warmth, and is to be seen in many an antique shop, brightly burnished and with an appropriate price tag (around £5 ($12) in the Home Counties of England). Little interest has so far been shown in the earthenware 'pig' hot-water bottle, which has also all but vanished from the scene, though there were many different forms of this type, and some are quite decorative.

On the subject of beds it should be noted that Victorian iron bedsteads, embellished with brass knobs and rails, are now fash-ionable again, duly transformed by several coats of white enamel paint.

The Victorian age witnessed the decline and eclipse of the horse-drawn carriage. The early years of the horseless carriage and other forms of motorized transport are dealt with in chapter

9, but under the heading of Victoriana one should mention the different types of cart and carriage used for the conveyance of people and things. Governess carts, landaus, broughams and jaunting-cars are but a few of the many kinds of carriage which are still surprisingly plentiful, though examples in good condition are now becoming very expensive. They have inspired quite a minor industry devoted to their restoration and renovation. Bigger items include caravans and mail-coaches, horse-drawn pantechnicons and farm-waggons, but here the problem of accommodation and space is a powerful deterrent to the would-be collector.

If the carriages themselves are too bulky for collecting, there are always the accessories which went with them. Coach lanterns are an old favourite, not only because of their decorative appearance but because they can easily be converted to electricity and used to illuminate porches and doorways. Saddlery and harness have their decorative uses, while horse brasses are perennial favourites (though one must beware of modern imitations die-stamped from sheet brass instead of cast or wrought as the originals were).

Metal fittings, undercarriages, door panels and cartwheels are all well worth looking out for, for decoration either inside or outside the house. Old boots in general may not appeal to the collector, but the elaborately constructed and heavily padded boots worn by postilions are much sought after and are rare in good condition. Spurs and stirrups may be found in many different varieties; all are collectable and have a considerable following nowadays.

Small vehicles are in great demand, since they take up less room, and are therefore more practicable as collectors' pieces. In this category come tradesmen's hand-carts, which are especially desirable if the original sign has been preserved to some degree. At a sale of Victoriana held in January 1969 Messrs King and Chasemore of Pulborough sold a nineteenth-century baker's hand-cart for £15 ($36). An interesting item which turned up in Hampshire recently was a dog-cart inscribed with the royal arms and believed to have been used in Victorian times for the delivery of mail—though there seems to have been some controversy over whether dogs were actually employed by the Post Office for this purpose. Victorian perambulators with high wickerwork backs and large wheels, not forgetting dolls' carriages, which were similar but smaller, are worth hunting for, and it is surprising how many attics and lumber-rooms in old houses still manage to yield up these treasures.

Early bicycles have long been in great demand, but with the

growing interest in 'veteran' bicycle rallies in recent years the value of early machines in good condition has soared enormously. The Victorian age was the era of the penny-farthing bicycle, so-called on account of its giant front wheel and diminutive rear wheel. Their humble name belies the value to which they have now risen, and one would be unlikely to find a reasonable example for less than £100 ($240) today. Other types of bicycle had begun to appear in the nineteenth century; the aptly named bone-shaker of the 1870s was more like the modern bicycle in appearance if not in refinements and comfort. Although it does not look quite as 'antique' as the penny-farthing, the bone-shaker is beginning to approach it in market value—a sign that the diminishing availability of the penny-farthing is tending towards the promotion of the next best. And so, in turn, the velocipedes, velocettes and other patent bicycles of the turn of the century are advancing in value, although, with their comparative plenitude, the scope for the collector is much wider. At a recent auction, for example, an unusual late-Victorian bicycle with a bamboo frame was knocked down for as little as £18 ($43). Admittedly it was in very poor condition, but in the judicious hands of the restorer this machine will undoubtedly repay that initial investment handsomely. Unusual machines, such as tandems, tricycles and quadricycles, rate a premium when they turn up. Similarly, children's bicycles and tricycles of a bygone age are worth hunting for. Probably because they were liable to suffer greater wear and tear at the hands of their youthful owners, these machines are exceedingly difficult to find in good condition, so here again careful restoration can pay handsome dividends.

Apart from coach lanterns, already referred to, the lighting equipment of the Victorian era provides a rich field for the collector. The early types of ordinary lanterns had windows of horn instead of glass and a tiny dormer window at the top for letting out the smoke. These 'lanthorns' are now rather expensive and, on account of their age (they died out in the 1840s), many may now be classed as antiques in the true sense. Their successors, however, with bottle-glass windows, have been used down to fairly recent times and are relatively plentiful: they are popular today either as decorative items *per se* or wired for electric light.

Candlesticks of all styles and periods are not uncommon, and Victorian examples in brass, electroplate, hardwood or pewter—not to mention the more exotic and expensive articles in gold or silver—can easily be found at prices ranging from a pound or two upwards. With the present vogue for soft candlelight as a prerequisite of fine wining and dining, Victorian candlesticks have been given a new lease of life in their original function. Many others, however, have been converted into small lamps for the table or mantelpiece.

Oil lamps are also avidly collected. The earliest types, with a separate reservoir, belong to the Regency period and are therefore outside the scope of this book. Parlour lamps, with the oil reservoir directly under the wick, began to appear in the early years of Victoria's reign and, with minor improvements and subtle developments, remained in use until superseded by electric lighting. These lamps vary considerably in shape, styling and materials used. Most of them favoured a long glass chimney to heighten the draught, but squat, dumpy versions, or round lamps with globular shades are also to be found. There were even standard oil lamps on brass or wrought-iron stands. These lamps were manufactured in all sorts of materials: apart from iron, bronze and brass, they may be found in porcelain, earthenware or stoneware, in pewter, pinchbeck, silver or even gold. The glass shades also vary considerably, from plain circular ones to those with delicate engraving and cutting. Moulded and pressed glass in numerous shapes and designs was also employed, and some of the highly distinctive types of glass which may be encountered are dealt with in greater detail in chapter 3.

Victorian office equipment, strange as it may seem, has suddenly become fashionable, and quite high prices are being paid in auction sales for the more interesting or unusual items. Perhaps the interest in these stems from a reaction against the rather uninspiring appearance, the streamlining and the stainless steel of so much modern office furniture and equipment. At any rate, few will deny that the odd item, such as a Victorian paperknife, leather-bound ink blotter or writing stand, adds a touch of charm and quaintness. Some readers may point out that they do not require these Victorian touches and that, thanks to the parsimony of their employers, the offices they work in are positively Dickensian. As a matter of interest, I took a critical look round the offices of the department of the British Museum in which I work. It is not so long ago, I am told, that a cupboard full of quill-pens was cleared out. Still doing sterling work are some Civil Service-issue paper knives whose leather scabbards bear the crowned monogram used in Victoria's time. Several leather-covered iron paperweights of the same vintage are also in use, and one of the secretaries has a fine example in bright yellow majolica with a bust of Queen Victoria and an inscription commemorating her Diamond Jubilee. The general office next door has a string-box of a type seldom met with these days, while the post-room boasts a candle stand and sealing equipment of indeterminate antiquity. Elsewhere in the building one finds wrought-iron hat stands and ornately embellished umbrella racks. These items, in short, are themselves museum pieces, though they are in everyday use. It has been suggested facetiously that the Museum should establish a Department of Museology in order to preserve these relics. Perhaps this is not such a bad idea, when one realizes that they now have some antiquarian value!

An indispensable piece of office equipment is the paper-clip. Most people, familiar only with the modern clip of curved wire, are unaware of the fact that the Victorian version is a highly collectable object. Seventy years ago paper clips were huge, spring-loaded affairs, die-stamped in many fancy designs out of sheets of steel, brass, copper or even silver. They were thus not as expendable as the present-day version, and a sheaf of papers held in their vice-like grip was well held indeed. The Victorian love of the ornate was extended to the most utilitarian items of office equipment: filing cabinets, letter racks, desks and swivel-chairs may all be found with lavish ornamental scrollwork. Fortunate the 'lady-typewriter' of Victorian times who wore long skirts; her modern, mini-skirted counterpart would be for ever laddering her tights in such baroque surroundings. Office automation, however, has been around rather longer than one might suppose. The first type-writers were, in fact, patented in the United States in 1868, so that the very earliest models now qualify for that over-worked epithet of antique. By the 1880s the telephone was an increasingly common feature in both homes and offices. Early hand-sets, in lacquered and gilded metal, are highly popular nowadays, not so much for use as telephones but for conversion into lamps or table-lighters.

The fashionable Victorian lady's dressing table was just as cluttered as that of her granddaughter, but in many respects it was much more fascinating. Hair brushes and hand looking glasses were elaborately ornamented, either in silver or ivory inlay, or with floridly decorated porcelain mounts. There were numerous small boxes serving a wide variety of purposes, as containers for hair pins, face powder, trinkets, jewelry or those sachets of lavender which were an indispensable feature of the Victorian boudoir. Scent bottles, both the table variety with built-in spray device and the small type intended for the purse, are avidly collected nowadays. Every technique of glass manufacture was used in their production, the glass being pressed, moulded, blown, cut or engraved. Different types of glass were used, from plain, clear glass to coloured glass of many hues, from opaline and vaseline glass to

Nailsea blue and marble slag glass. Here is a field which is full of promise, the commercial scent bottles of the period up to about the First World War being both plentiful and cheap, though interest in glass generally is such that prices are beginning to rise. Scent bottles intended for the reticule or purse were treated almost like jewelry, and much care and craftsmanship was lavished on them. They are usually found with silver caps (whose hallmarks should enable the collector to date them accurately), and these were covered with decorative motifs. Double scent bottles, with stoppers at both ends, were intended to serve two purposes. One compartment contained perfume, while the other held the smelling salts which the Victorian lady found so necessary. Tight-corsetting and the fetid, oil-lit atmosphere combined to make 'attacks of the vapours' a common occurrence.

The double scent bottle was the successor to the vinaigrette, a small box usually made of silver and not unlike a snuff box in outward appearance. Inside, however, was a hinged, perforated grille enclosing an inner compartment which was gold-plated. The gilding gives some clue to the contents of the box—a piece of sponge soaked in a strong (and highly corrosive) solution of aromatic vinegar. This liquid, which overpowered bad smells as much as it revived the faint, was devised in the 1780s by a Dr William Henry, and it was largely as a result of his lectures on the subject of public health and hygiene that vinaigrettes became so fashionable in the later years of the eighteenth century. Dr Henry's Vinegar was originally intended to have a prophylactic effect—to prevent contagion with infectious diseases and epidemics. Gradually, however, its formula changed, and a generation or so later it was being used more as a pick-me-up. While the heyday of the vinaigrette was well and truly in the antique period, it should be noted that these charming trifles were popular—with the older generation at least—as late as 1900, and there are many attractive examples which fall within the Victorian era. The decoration on vinaigrettes was often extremely elaborate, with *repoussé* work, *guilloché* or engine-turning, piercing and embossing in handsome floral or geometric patterns. Vinaigrettes may still be picked up for a few pounds, but examples with scenery (particularly castles and churches) on their lids may rate ten times that sum or even more.

POT LIDS

In the realm of cosmetics there are many objects which are now eminently collectable. The jars which held creams, unguents and pomades were often fine examples of contemporary ceramic art, but attention is usually confined to their lids, which were generally embellished with pictures, transfer-printed in up to four colours and sometimes surrounded by a gold border. Pot lids or pomade tops have long been popular with collectors—their attractive appearance must have encouraged people to keep rather than discard them when the contents of the jars were expended. They seem to have originated in the 1840s and were used originally on jars of bear's grease (known also as pomatum or pomade), a form of hairdressing which was borrowed from the North American Indians and became popular after men's wigs went out of fashion. It is for this reason that many of the earlier examples of pomade tops have pictures showing bears in various whimsical poses. Pictorial pot lids were used for a wide variety of cosmetic preparations —creams, ointments and even toothpaste—and the manufacturers of these commodities seem to have been at great pains to ensure that their goods were packaged as artistically as possible. They showed beautiful ladies in exotic poses or reproduced in miniature paintings such as Gainsborough's 'Blue Boy' and the works of contemporary artists such as Landseer, Mulready and Wilkie.

Pictorial pot lids were mainly used, however, for fish and meat paste jars—hence the prevalence of nautical subjects in their design. It was the fashion for Pegwell Bay shrimps in the 1850s which gave the pot lid its greatest impetus. The majority of pictorial pot lids were produced by four Staffordshire potteries: Mayer Brothers and Elliot, Ridgeway of Cauldon, Ridgeway of Shelton and F. and F. Pratt of Fenton. Of these the lids produced by the last-named are the most sought after by collectors. The success of this firm was largely due to the inventive genius of Felix Pratt, who in 1847 patented 'improvements in the manufacture of cylindrical articles composed of earthenware', and to the technical brilliance of Jesse Austin, who developed the process for four-colour printing.

Pratts were commissioned by the two leading fish-paste manufacturers, Tatnell and Sons and S. Banger, to produce pictorial lids for them. This venture was apparently a huge success, demonstrated by the large number of Pegwell Bay pot lids still in existence. Pictorial pot lids might never have risen above the mundane nature of the goods they enclosed were it not for the Great Exhibition of 1851, at which the pot lid manufacturers displayed their wares. They broke away from the nautical *genre* on this occasion by producing pot lids showing the Grand International Building and other views of the exhibition.

The International Exhibition of 1862, L'Exposition Universelle of 1867 and the Columbian Exposition of 1893 were also commemorated in this way. The exhibition pot lids are fairly plentiful, and range in value from about £10 ($24) for the commonest views to about £50 ($120) or more for scarce examples of the Columbian Exposition. The Great Exhibition also encouraged the production of pot lids with purely artistic motifs, and some of these, such as the Strawberry Girl and the Hop Queen, framed in a gold band, are now worth £100 ($240) to £200. These attractive designs paved the way for the wide variety of pot lids portraying contemporary personalities (from the Duke of Wellington to Jenny Lind), topical events such as the battles of the Crimean War, animals, scenery and Shakespearean subjects.

The production of pictorial pot lids went into decline in the last quarter of the nineteenth century, partly because of the diminishing popularity of potted shrimps but mainly because of the death of Jesse Austin in 1879. Pratts ceased manufacturing pictorial pot lids in 1880, and gradually the other potteries followed suit, though the food manufacturers, Crosse and Blackwell, maintained the tradition to the end of the century. Shortly after Felix Pratt's death in 1894 a large quantity of remainders came on the market, and it is from that date that the collecting of pot lids really commenced. In 1924 Messrs Puttick and Simpson held the first auction of pictorial pot lids, and the surprisingly high prices paid for some of them showed that they had definitely become collectors' pieces. At that time the record auction price for a single pot lid was the £50 paid in 1924 for Pratt's 'The Buffalo Hunt'. The latest auction record, at the time of writing, is £130 ($312) paid at a Puttick sale for 'Harriet Beecher Stowe' in 1969. Mounted in circular frames, these lids make an attractive and more enduring substitute for miniatures as wall decoration.

DRESS ACCESSORIES

Returning to the boudoir, however, there are numerous other items, apart from cosmetic jars and their lids, which are now of interest to the collector. Jars in glass or porcelain, often highly decorative, were also used for face powder. Often they had a powder puff backed by the same material and mounted in silver incorporated in the lid. As ladies' purses and handbags became more capacious such items as lipsticks and powder compacts became increasingly common. The early types, used from the last years of the Victorian era onwards, are quite scarce—mainly because it was regarded as indecent to redden one's lips, and no self-respecting lady would be seen in public looking in a mirror, far less powdering her nose. Portable cosmetics for the handbag really date from Edwardian times and did not become fashionable to a great extent till the twenties. As their popularity increased, however, gold compacts were given as expensive presents on special occasions, and though this custom has largely died out, these beautiful examples of the goldsmith's art survive, standing favourable comparison with the enamelled and jeweled trifles of the eighteenth century, though they are not yet desired so highly by the collectors of today.

Victorian gentlemen required more dress accessories than their modern counterparts: thus we find stud boxes in leather, ivory, hardwood, porcelain or silver, collar and glove boxes in leather, wood or silver, or watchstands and trees on which the large pocket watches of the period could be placed at night. Watchstands come in a wide variety of shapes, some of them quite fantastic in appearance. They were usually made in brass, though the better quality ones also existed in silver. The early watchstands, produced in the eighteenth century, are now very rare and exceedingly expensive when they turn up in the auction room, but the Victorian examples, produced as late as the First World War, are more plentiful and still quite reasonably priced.

Glove stretchers, shoe horns, button hooks, hair tongs and curlers, are but a few of the other objects to be found in the Victorian bedroom or dressing room. Here again a wide variety of materials were used, and invariably the handles were ornately decorated. Etuis—cases for manicure or sewing sets—had their heyday in the late eighteenth century, but attractive examples embellished with piqué work or inlaid with silver or ivory were produced until the end of the nineteenth century. Sets of scissors, nail file, cuticle knife, nail buffer and other manicure implements are, of course, still being manufactured, but few of them possess the decorative qualities which distinguished those of sixty years ago. Victorian thimbles, in materials ranging from gold or silver to minutely decorated porcelain, are eagerly collected nowadays and have the advantage of being very compact and easy to house.

Dress accessories range from the richly carved wooden stay-busks, which were popular at the beginning of Victoria's reign, to buckles and buttons of all kinds. The stay-busk was a flat strip of wood inserted into the front of the stays or corset in order to achieve the 'flat tummy' effect which women (in Europe at any rate) have always considered so desirable. Stay-busks were acceptable as presents from husbands and sweethearts and, as love tokens, they were often decorated with hearts, lovers' knots and other symbols of affection. A large collection of stay-busks was formed by Edward Pinto and is now preserved in the Birmingham Museum and Art Gallery.

Buttons may at first seem too prosaic a subject for the collector, but rummage through grandma's button box and you will soon discover what a wealth of material is offered. Apart from the common shirt button made of horn, ivory or mother of pearl, there are the more exotic varieties with jeweled or paste tops. Buttons on the breast and sleeves of coats, jackets and dresses were produced in literally a myriad forms. The most expensive were of gold or silver (if the latter was used, inlays of gold were often employed) delicately engraved or beaten with intricate patterns, mythological figures or scenery. Some buttons of French origin had tiny pictures, transfer-printed in multicolour and covered with glass. Every technique of the jeweler's and metalworker's art was employed in the manufacture of buttons, so the scope for the collector is truly enormous. Among the unusual types one sometimes finds coins mounted as buttons. Buttons engraved or die-stamped with noble coats of arms may have come from the livery of footmen. Regimental buttons are a vast subject in themselves and, of course, they are still being produced today. The true collectors' pieces, however, are the buttons bearing the insignia of units and formations which have long ceased to exist. The period from the Crimea to the First World War is particularly fruitful, with emphasis on the many formations of an ephemeral nature which flourished briefly during the Boer War (1899–1902).

Pins of various sorts are also collectable, and although brooches and *fibulae* had been in existence for centuries as dress fasteners, the pin as we know it today only emerged in the 1840s following the invention in the United States of a rotary machine for wire-drawing and pin manufacturing. Hat pins, hair pins, safety pins and plain ordinary pins were produced in the nineteenth century in a profusion of decorative styles. Not only were such mundane articles as safety pins decorated carefully but they were also made of silver or gold—so fine examples may be lying around unconsidered for their true value. Hat pins naturally have always had more ornament lavished on them than any other type of pin, and a large and varied collection can be put together for a reasonable sum. While on the subject of hat pins I should mention hat pin holders, which are also worth collecting. They were produced in different metals and may also be found in glass, pottery or porcelain. Some of the last-named type have fetched quite high prices, depending on the quality of the decoration and the name of the pottery concerned.

Buckles on belts and shoes were made in many different materials from gold and silver to brass, ivory, cloth-covered steel and wood. Here again the variety of decorative forms is immense. More intriguing, perhaps, is the amount of decoration which the Victorians apparently liked to have on the buckles of garters, suspenders, braces and other items not exposed to the gaze of the idle bystander. Stocking garters were in use until the advent of the suspender in the later years of the nineteenth century, and as an accessory of some erotic significance have never quite died out, though in a purely functional sense they are unnecessary. Garters, surprisingly enough, were regarded as acceptable presents from men to women, and not necessarily only between lovers. The gift of stockings and garters was common practice in the seventeenth and eighteenth centuries as part of the festival of St Valentine's Day, when one's Valentine was taken to be the first young lady seen on that morning—and not necessarily one's lady love. This charming custom had already begun to die out, even before Victorian prudery killed it stone dead. Nevertheless, garters and their buckles continued to be highly decorative, and some examples dating from the 'Naughty Nineties' would be considered rather daring even today.

POSTCARDS

In the field of ephemera Victoriana reigns supreme. The graphic arts received a tremendous fillip during this period, and there is absolutely no comparison between the layout and lettering adopted in advertisements at the beginning of this period with that in general use by the end of the century. The early examples may have been crude and full of shortcomings technically, but they possess none the less a certain naïveté and charm which makes them appeal to the collector.

Other forms of Victorian ephemera include trade cards, decorated note paper, Valentines, Christmas cards and picture postcards. Each has a large band of devotees, and a considerable literature now exists dealing with special aspects of them. Since small ephemera of this sort are perhaps the most easily collected form of Victoriana, it is hardly surprising that they have attracted such a large following. Consequently, the market in these items is more stable (though prices are rising all the time), and even though new finds of scrapbooks, albums and bundles of correspondence are always coming to light, the demand is definitely outpacing the supply. Not so long ago, for example, one could pick up old postcard albums for 10s ($1.20), and many a junk dealer would have a box of assorted postcards priced at 1d (1¢) each. I was able to pick up many interesting and (as it turns out) quite rare cards for this modest sum in the junk-shops of Glasgow and Birmingham. I was shocked—indeed, outraged—to find similar accumulations in the Portobello Road area of London priced at sixpence each. All this was ten years ago, and I fear that the junk dealers of the Midlands and north of England have got wise to the ways of collectors and priced such stocks as they retain accordingly. As for the London market in picture postcards, it has become refined and sophisticated beyond recognition. Instead of the battered shoe-boxes of yesteryear, with their haphazard collections of cards, there are filing cabinets containing trays labelled Trains, Actresses, Comic, Ships, Military, Royalty, etc., and scenic postcards are classified into county and alphabetical order. With such regimentation aiding the specialist collector, the demand is channelled immediately towards the available supply. No longer is it possible to dip at random and pick out the unconsidered trifle; cards are priced on an accurate, almost scientific basis, and the rise of the specialist dealer means that there are now fewer bargains around for the knowledgeable collector to profit by.

Picture postcards were invented by an Austrian in 1869, so the earliest Continental examples are now qualifying as antiques. Oddly enough, although Britain adopted the postcard in the following year, the Post Office forbade the use of pictorial embellishment until 1894. Even then, the regulations stipulated that nothing other than the address could appear on the back of the card, so that in the early British examples the picture on the front occupies only a portion of that side, the rest being allocated for the message. Gradually, however, the picture came to occupy a more prominent space, and the message or conventional greeting was reduced to the margin. At the turn of the century the regulations were relaxed and the back of the postcard was divided equally between the message and the address.

Technically the picture postcards of the late Victorian and Edwardian periods in England were rather poor. Printed in vast quantities (Saxony had a large industry devoted to the export of scenic postcards covering the entire world), they were sold very cheaply—at a halfpenny each, while packets of a dozen were even cheaper. Since second class postage was also very cheap (the postage on a card up to February 1918 was a halfpenny—half the letter rate), people followed the example set by the canny Mr Gladstone and sent postcards instead of letters. Postcards were not only cheap but quick and, in an age before the telephone was common, people sent postcards for all manner of reasons, many of them quite trivial. The postcard albums of the pre-First World War period are fascinating social documents, not only for the interest contained in the pictures of Victorian and Edwardian Britain but for the messages inscribed on them. Picture postcards gained enormously in popularity in Edwardian times, and by the outbreak of the First World War the Post Office was handling an estimated 50 million every week. The doubling of the postcard rate in 1918 (for a short time immediately after the war it was actually trebled) was a heavy blow to its popularity and, with the attendant rise in production costs, people got out of the postcard habit. It has survived to this day, but is more or less confined to the tourist souvenir of holiday resorts, and in the years since the Second World War there has been a noticeable improvement in the glossy, multicoloured appearance of the picture postcard. Now that it is possible to send second class mail in a sealed envelope the postcard has no advantage over the letter except as a souvenir of places visited. It will be interesting to see whether the introduction of the two-tier postage system in Britain will have any marked effect on the volume of picture postcards sent by tourists and holidaymakers. If the picture postcard were to vanish from the scene the criterion of obsolescence would automatically transmute it into a 'bygone', but at the moment only the cards of the pre-1914 era can be regarded as having any antiquarian value.

There is a subtle link between the picture postcard and the other two major types of postal ephemera, since in the Edwardian heyday of the postcard both Christmas cards and Valentines were sent in this form to a very large extent. This was the era of the comic or satirical Valentine, and its public transmission in postcard form no doubt contributed to the chagrin and embarrassment of the recipient.

VALENTINES

Valentines themselves had a much older history than the picture postcard and originated in the age-old customs attending the Festival of St Valentine. This obscure third-century martyr was executed in Rome on 14 February AD 270, which date coincided with the eve of the Lupercalia, an ancient pagan festival involving fertility rites and traditionally celebrated in connection with the return of spring. Like Christmas and Easter, the celebrations of which were grafted on to older pagan festivals, St Valentine's Day became inextricably linked with the spring festival when 'a young man's fancy lightly turns to thoughts of love'.

For centuries St Valentine's Day was celebrated as an occasion for exchanging gifts and tokens of affection. From about 1760 onwards, however, the giving of expensive presents to one's Valentine became the exception rather than the rule, and instead it was customary to give a prettily written letter. To assist the lover in his romantic composition there were numerous volumes of suitable verses and manuals of complimentary phrases. Gradually these *billets doux* came to be lavishly decorated with lovers' knots, cupid's bows, hearts and other symbols of affection. Early examples of these Valentines, with hand-drawn or painted pictures, intricate pin-prick and cut-out work or collages of lace, silk and thread, are now greatly prized by collectors.

Printed Valentines followed hard on the heels of pictorial writing paper, which was introduced in the last decade of the eighteenth century. Some of these early printed Valentines were engraved by Francesco Bartolozzi and have long been in demand by collectors of Bartolozzi prints. By 1803 H. Dobbs and Co. were established as fancy paper manufacturers and had begun the production of Valentines on a commercial scale. Dobbs' Valentines were renowned for their superb decoration and intricate embossing, and on account of the constant changes to the firm's imprint it is possible to date such items fairly closely. The earliest and scarcest are those inscribed DOBBS PATENT. The production of embossed and die-stamped Valentines had been reduced to a fine art by the middle of the nineteenth century. In 1834 Joseph Addenbrooke devised a method of simulating a lace effect in paper, and Valentines produced in the ensuing decades were noted for the intricacy of their decoration, several layers of paper lace being quite common.

Even before the advent of cheap postage in 1840 the sending of Valentines had reached formidable proportions, some 60,000 additional letters being transmitted in the London Twopenny Post alone on St Valentine's Day 1834. At this time the method of computing postage was according to the number of sheets, and the use of an envelope doubled the charge. Thus Valentines, complete with ornate lacy envelopes, dating before 1840 are exceedingly rare. The use of special Valentine envelopes increased in popularity after 1840 and the introduction of Uniform Penny Postage, but Victorian Valentines, up to about 1870, with matching envelope, are worth a considerable premium, since they appeal to postal historians as much as to collectors of Victoriana. Fine examples of this sort may be worth as much as £50 ($120), and the bidding is usually keen when they turn up in Robson Lowe Postal History auctions.

Comic Valentines, often of a malicious nature, became increasingly popular in the latter half of the nineteenth century. The advent of the picture postcard, as already mentioned, popularized and cheapened the Valentine even further. This, in a sense, was its undoing, for the cheap joke Valentines of the Edwardian era put an end to the serious nature of Valentine's Day customs. Edwardian Valentines in postcard form were sent by the million, and thousands of them have been preserved in the postcard albums of the period. Dealers in ephemera can generally supply examples at prices from a few shillings upwards. The custom of sending Valentines died out in Britain with the First World War, but it was revived in 1926 when Raphael Tuck launched a Valentine campaign to mark their centenary as card manufacturers. Ten years later the Valentine even received official recognition when the General Post Office instituted the Valentine greetings telegram, and the habit of sending Valentines has gone from strength to strength ever since. From a collector's viewpoint the only Valentines worth bothering about are the ornate Victorian examples, though the more vindictive of the Edwardian ones have a perverted charm which some people find appealing.

CHRISTMAS CARDS

In view of the antiquity of the Valentine, it is strange that the Christmas card should be of comparative youth. It is, in fact, only within the past hundred years that they have been manufactured on a commercial scale (since the establishment in 1867 of the London branch of the printing and publishing business founded by Marcus Ward). Mr Ward was the first publisher to develop the Christmas card industry beyond the somewhat dilettante approach of his predecessors. Great attention was paid to design, and the leading artists of the time were commissioned to illustrate the cards. Among the designers whose work is immortalized in the cards of Marcus Ward were Walter Crane, H. Stacy Marks and, of course, Kate Greenaway. Miss Greenaway's over-dressed Victorian children enjoyed a tremendous popularity in the 1870s and 1880s, and Christmas cards designed by her now fetch comparatively high prices. It is recorded that she herself received as little as three guineas for a design in the early years, although two sets of original drawings, produced by her for Christmas cards, fetched over £20 ($48) at auction as long ago as 1884.

Christmas cards had been in existence for at least a generation before 1867, however, and examples from the embryonic period are extremely scarce and highly prized nowadays. Some controversy has raged over the question of the first Christmas card, but it is now generally accepted that this honour is due to the card designed by John Horsley and published at Felix Summerly's Home Treasury Office in Bond Street, London. The date of this card has long been disputed, but has now been definitely assigned to 1843. Summerly's Home Treasury was a project sponsored by Sir Henry Cole, to whom many give the credit for inventing the Christmas card. Personally I am not so sure. It would seem surprising that greetings cards should have existed for St Valentine's Day and not for Christmas at an earlier date; and the existence of such a Christmas card in the Dickens Papers, recently deposited at the British Museum, would seem to prove that their antiquity is greater than has hitherto been suspected. This card, inscribed 'A Merry Christmas' is preserved with its envelope, and the superscription on it indicates that it was sent to Dickens at Christmastide 1835.

The Cole–Horsley card was lithographed by Lobbins of Warwick Court, Holborn, London, and hand-coloured by a professional 'colourer' named Mason.

The cards were sold for 1s (12¢) each, and it has been estimated that fewer than a thousand were sold. Of these, barely a dozen are now known to exist, and most of them are in the United States, where the collecting of Christmas cards has always been more strongly developed than in Britain. One of these cards was purchased by a friend of mine in a London shop for £5 ($12) some twenty years ago: today it would find a ready buyer for over £100 ($240).

The design of the Cole–Horsley card seems quaint by modern standards. No one could object to the subjects of the side panels, which represented the spirit of Christmas charity, but the main vignette, depicting a large Victorian family toasting the absent friend (the addressee) with glasses of red wine, was severely censured at the time as being an incitement to drunkenness! Ironically, Horsley, in his later years, earned a certain notoriety as the Royal Academician who denounced nude modelling; for this he was nicknamed 'Clothes' Horsley.

There were other Christmas cards in the 1840s (that produced by W.M. Egley having been a serious contender for the title of the first, on account of the difficulty in deciphering the date, 1848, printed on it), but their popularity was restricted for many years. Many of the cards in the 'classic' period were made and printed by hand. They developed slowly alongside the more popular Christmas notepaper and envelopes. These envelopes were often gaily decorated and had ornately embossed flaps which could be cut out and mounted on plain card. In this way the mid-Victorian Christmas card composed of scraps on several layers of embossed and perforated paper gradually evolved. Examples of these cards, from the 1850s and 1860s, scarcely larger than a playing card and intricately decorated with lace, silk ribbons or scraps, are very scarce (especially with matching envelopes), though it is still possible to pick them up for a few pounds. Animated cards, which were in vogue for a time in the period 1870–80, are now expensive if in good condition, and a complicated example may fetch up to £20 ($48).

The development of the techniques of die-sinking and embossing encouraged C. Goodall & Son to manufacture Christmas cards on a commercial basis in 1862, but in face of the competition from Marcus Ward they turned to other and more lucrative forms of publishing. Marcus Ward, in turn, gave way to Raphael Tuck & Sons, whose first Christmas cards were published in 1871. Raphael Tuck promoted the Christmas card with public design competitions offering vast sums of prize money, and held regular exhibitions of the season's new designs. Tremendous impetus was given to the habit of sending Christmas cards by the introduction of the postal regulation of 1870 permitting postcards; the few thousands which passed through the post in the 1860s swelled to as many millions by the end of the century.

Post-1870 Christmas cards can still be picked up for a few shillings unless they happen to be of special interest. Victorian scrapbooks and albums are the most likely source of early Christmas cards and Valentines, but they are rapidly disappearing from the junk shops and second-hand bookshops. Several London dealers now specialize in small ephemera for the collector, the best of these being John Hall of Knightsbridge, Them and Theirs of St Christopher's Place, off Oxford Street, and Pleasures of Past Times (David Drummond) of Cecil Court, off Charing Cross Road.

AMERICANA

Much the same pattern is repeated in the United States, but the history of that country in the past century or so has resulted in the collecting of 'Victoriana' taking a narrower, more extreme form, both in the period covered and in the range of subjects now considered collectable. Industrialization, on the same scale as in Britain, did not reach the United States till the 1870s, but development was so intense and rapid from then onwards that on the eve of the First World War it was the most highly industrialized country in the world. America today has the most sophisticated consumer society in the world, but this position may, in fact, have been reached as early as 1900. A comparison of mail order catalogues in Britain and the United States of this period shows that the range and diversity of goods available to the consumer in the latter country was larger, perhaps because the spending power of the average worker's wages was much greater even then.

The population of the United States expanded phenomenally in the half century following the Civil War. In 1869 it stood at 39 millions: by 1890 it had risen to 63 millions, and in 1915 it had reached 100 millions. Immigration as well as a rising birth rate contributed to this phenomenal growth. Today the population of the United States stands at 200 millions—five times that of 1869. Since the America of a century ago had very limited resources in the way of furniture, ceramics, metalware and *objets d'art*, it follows that the vast army of American collectors must look elsewhere for material. In the colonial period, up to 1776, the American middle and upper classes imported luxury goods from Europe, principally from Britain, though even at this early date there was a flourishing indigenous body of arts, crafts and manufacture in America. Today articles which have survived for two centuries or more, both imported British and locally manufactured goods, are invariably preserved in museums. Very little of it is ever available to the general collecting public, whose insatiable demand far outpaced the supply many years ago.

Americans in general have been at the collecting game for longer than anyone else; their comparatively high income and relatively shorter working hours gave them the time and the wherewithal to take up a collecting hobby a couple of decades before Britain and certainly long before France, Germany or Italy. Even now, when the collecting mania has become well-developed in Western Europe, it is seldom pursued as intensely as in America, which has more stamp collectors, coin collectors and antique hunters per head of population than any other country in the world.

To meet the voracious demand for 'collectables' Americans have for years been combing the antique and junk shops of the Old World to redress the material balance of the New. Important collections of European antiques were, of course, formed before the

First World War and between the wars. But these were in the hands of the millionaire collectors: Carnegie and Mellon immediately spring to mind. The post-Second World War phenomenon of collecting European material on a vast popular scale started in about 1946 with the return of the GIs who had liberated Western Europe. Since then there has been a steady stream of antique—and not so antique—material flowing westward across the Atlantic. The American Invasion, as it is often called, has had a marked effect in Britain on the availability of material—not to mention the price, which has rocketed in the case of many items which at one time would have been considered totally lacking in antiquarian interest.

This brings me to the second, and more significant, factor in American collecting habits. Since only a small proportion of American collectors can manage the transatlantic trip to hunt for material in Europe, the vast majority of them have been forced to collect objects available in their own country. Because material in the true antique sense is not plentiful, objects of a much later period have been promoted to the status of collectors' pieces. One can readily understand the interest and collectability of relatively modern glass, ceramics and silverware which are examples of fine craftsmanship despite their relative youth. But what seems astonishing is the interest shown in quite mundane objects of the late nineteenth and early twentieth centuries. This preoccupation with the everyday material of the immediate past may be justified by the pace at which the world around us is changing. A century ago, when mankind progressed relatively slowly, it was sufficient for scholars and collectors to be preoccupied with the remains of ancient civilizations, with the worlds of Egypt, of Greece and Rome. Nowadays the progress of civilization is so meteoric that one's way of life may be completely outmoded in a decade or even a year. Thus history is no longer thousands or hundreds of years ago but last year or last week. In this age of instant history the material objects of the immediate past begin to assume an aura of antiquity which would have been impossible twenty years ago. This may sound ridiculous, but is it? Every day I pass the gates of RAF Northolt, and am always struck by the quaint, other-worldly appearance of the Spitfire which is preserved there as a memorial of the Battle of Britain. Yet barely twenty-five years ago this museum piece was the most advanced fighter aircraft in the world. If the Russians have preserved the first sputniks in museums they must seem positively antique alongside the giant inter-planetary Soyuz spacecraft of today—and yet it is barely ten years since the first satellite was put into orbit.

40

Remember also that America has the consumer society *par excellence*, where last year's model is on today's scrap-heap, and you can begin to appreciate how objects of fairly recent vintage can be regarded as almost antique. In his latest book, *The Coming Collecting Boom*, John Mebane discusses an astonishing range of items which are beginning to attract the attention of American collectors. They include the following: apple parers, bib holders, dolls' furniture, babies' rattles and teething rings, barrels, chamber-pots, bells, biscuit tins, bread boards, butter boxes, can openers, cigar boxes, cash registers, door knobs, coat hangers, coffee grinders, corkscrews, curtain rings and poles, drawer handles, duplicating machines, fish scales, fly catchers, fruit jars, frying pans, gambling apparatus, hooks of all kinds, ice picks, inkwells, key chains and rings, lemon squeezers, meat cleavers, mechanical banks, mucilage bottles, moustache combs, oil cans, paper clips, pencil sharpeners, Pepsi Cola trays, pickle jars, potato mashers, rice boilers, rolling pins, rowing machines, sand buckets, sardine shears, school bags, screw cases, sieves, skewers, slot machines, stair rods and buttons, stamp moisteners, staple fasteners, thermometers, towel rails, transom catches and undertakers' hardware.

The oddest of all collectable items seems to me to be barbed wire, to which Mr Mebane devotes an entire chapter. To understand the interest, history and romance surrounding such an apparently utilitarian subject it is necessary to remember that the American Wild West was tamed by the stuff. Although a form of barbed wire had been invented in France, it was not until 1873 that an American, Henry M. Rose, patented a kind of wire fencing which was subsequently developed and improved by Joseph Glidden and Isaac Ellwood. Barbed wire was initially used by the 'nesters' and homesteaders to protect their arable land from marauding cattle. The cattlemen bitterly resented the wire, which symbolized the end to their free-ranging activities, but eventually came to realize that it would also be useful to them. Many different types and patterns of wire have been recorded: Henry D. and Frances T. McCallum, in their book *The Wire that Fenced the West*, state that more than 400 types are known. The rarest and most eagerly sought types rejoice under such names as Meriweather's Snake, Reynolds' Hanging Knot, Kelly's Thorny Fence, Pooler Jones, Stover Clip and Concertina Steel. It is estimated that there are now more than 150,000 barbed wire collectors in the United States, and the hobby has dealers, collectors' clubs and quite a profuse literature testifying to its popularity. Wire is collected in lengths of 18 inches, and ranges in market value from $1 to $5 a 'stick'. The centre of this unusual hobby is, not surprisingly, located in Texas, where the 'antique shops' and ye olde trading posts do a roaring business in wire. The Texas Barbed Wire Collectors' Association publishes a monthly journal entitled *The Barbarian*—presumably this is meant as a pun and is not the actual name used to denote a collector of barbed wire.

2 Silver

The only material dealt with in this book which may be said to have an intrinsic value, even when antiquarian or aesthetic considerations are totally absent, is silver. Since the devaluation of sterling in November 1967, the British market for silver has leaped ahead of all others in the field of fine arts. Devaluation of 14 per cent was expected to lead to a 20 per cent increase in silver values; but by the end of the 1967–68 season dealers and auctioneers were reporting a general increase of 60 per cent in silver prices. While much of the turnover in the sale rooms and the dealers' shops is in antique silver, two new trends have become apparent in recent years. Victorian silver, despised not so long ago and usually regarded as being worth no more than its scrap value, has begun to acquire an antiquarian value. The other noticeable development is that good modern silver, formerly a buyer's market, is now turning into a seller's market.

Victorian silver is characterized, as is so much else from that ebullient era, by its extravagant and ostentatious use of decoration. It was the most important status symbol of the Victorian period, and for those who could afford it it was impossible to have too much of a good thing. When silver deposits were discovered in America and Australia in the early years of the century the output of the raw material increased enormously: it was thus possible to meet the demand created by rising prosperity in Britain, the United States and the countries of Western Europe. The invention of Sheffield plate in the 1760s was overshadowed a century later by the technique of electroplating, which brought 'silver' within the reach of all but the very poorest; but for anyone with any pretensions to wealth and social standing nothing but silver itself would suffice.

The period from 1830 to 1900 was therefore a boom time in the silver industry. The restrained classicism of the silver produced in the early decades of the century, exemplified by the earlier works

43

of Paul Storr, the Batemans, Rundle, Hemings, Hennell and other great artist-craftsmen of that era, gave way in the 1830s to the rococo revival. In place of the simple gadrooning and the Egyptian ornament (inspired by Napoleon's campaign in Egypt at the turn of the century) came the asymmetrical lines and scroll-work of the rococo style, but, as is so often the case in revivals, the craze for *rocaille* work was taken to extremes. The straightforward acanthus-leaf motif of Regency silver gave way to trailing vines and a veritable range of scrollwork, bases became massive and rock-like (a literal translation of the *rocaille* from which rococo was derived) and emphasis was laid on the weight or massy appearance of the object. This tendency for exaggeration in form and decoration pervaded the whole of mid-Victorian silverware, but was seen at its worst in the elaborate centrepieces and presentation items in which the Victorians took great delight. In the production of these testimonials in silver the designers really let themselves go: allegorical figures, heraldic devices and obscure symbolism were often combined in a hideous nightmare which almost screams at one, like the Podsnap plate in Dickens' *Our Mutual Friend*, 'Here you have as much of me in my ugliness as if I were only lead; but I am so many ounces of precious metal worth so much an ounce—wouldn't you like to melt me down?'

This is precisely what has happened to an untold quantity of Victorian 'decorative' silver over the past fifty years. The reaction against the sheer ugliness of these exuberant presentation pieces set in before the First World War, and only the bullion market showed any interest in them. Now all this has changed and, judging by recent (1969) prices in the auction rooms, such pieces are selling for at least twice the current bullion price of silver. It is interesting to note that this trend was apparent even before the sterling devaluation in November 1967: in August of that year it had already been estimated that Victorian pieces were fetching rather more than 30 per cent more than their scrap value. We must accept that Victorian silver centrepieces, figures and orna-mental ware now have an antiquarian value, though I suspect that this is rather artificial and dictated more by contemporary economic considerations than aesthetic criteria. Victorian useful wares—tea and coffee services, bowls, dishes, cutlery and the like—are in a somewhat different category. Fortunately the degree of ornamentation had to be limited by the element of functional-ism involved, so that these pieces did not suffer the unrestrained licence of the showpieces. Their very usefulness has helped to pre-serve them from the melting pot and given them a market value which has always managed to stay one jump ahead of the bullion price. Consequently, the proportion of domestic or useful wares which has survived is higher than that of the ornamental pieces, but demand for good, usable Victorian silver (which often blends surprisingly readily with the modern dining room) has always been fairly steady, satisfying the requirements of those who enjoy the pleasure of handling silver in everyday use but who cannot afford antique silver.

One cannot dismiss Victorian silver lightly, whether fussy centrepieces or less heavily decorated useful wares. The showy silver sculpture of centrepieces may possess some historical value, if the occasion of the testimonial or presentation is sufficiently important and not of purely ephemeral interest. But, personally, I feel that the event or person thus honoured would have to be very important to make the item worth collecting. In the more functional items one should not overlook the various attempts to break away from the stereotyped conventions, borrowing on the styles of past eras, which influenced silver design so overwhelmingly in the nineteenth century. One of these attempts, which stands out amid the florid dreariness of the period, was made by Henry Cole, whose Felix Summerly's Art Manufactures in the 1840s and 1850s produced some refreshingly simple designs for plates, mugs and bowls and, in a way, anticipated the Arts and Crafts movement of the 1880s. Cole and his colleagues strove to produce designs incorporating naturalistic ornament of a strictly 'appropriate' character, but they were too influenced, albeit perhaps unconsciously, by the styles prevalent at the time for their work to be entirely successful. Nevertheless, examples of the silverware produced under the auspices of Felix Summerly's Art Manufactures have a definite antiquarian interest, and their value seems assured.

One of Cole's associates was Matthew Digby Wyatt, who wrote, in *Metalwork and its Artistic Design* (1852),

'We may draw attention to two or three indisputable requisites to a good design for silversmith's work. In the first place, the object must be so formed as to fulfil the purpose for which it is intended: that object must in no way be disguised, but, on the contrary, should be apparent on the first cursory inspection; the general outline should be symmetrical and the disposition of the various parts as proportioned as to appear strong, and equal to the constructive duties they may be called upon to perform; the amount of ornament should be proportioned to the purpose of the object and the means and conditions of its proprietors; there should be no direct imitation of nature, and yet no perversion of her forms; and lastly, it would be well if a system of judicious contrast of plain surfaces and enrichment were carried throughout such works, and each ornament applied only to those points where the general form appears to demand accentuation.'

45

Theorizing such as this was admirable as far as it went, but it required the publicity of the Great Exhibition of 1851 and the subsequent international exhibitions and world fairs to draw the public's attention to the best (and the worst) in contemporary design. Arising directly out of the Great Exhibition, incidentally, was the foundation of what is now the Royal College of Art in London—one of the earliest of the great art schools of the world. Before the middle of the nineteenth century art was regarded as something one was born with and little was done to teach art as a subject. While it remains a matter for conjecture how far art can be instilled in the classroom, the art schools and colleges have certainly made an important contribution to the higher standards of craftsmanship and design which in recent years have become evident in all the applied arts. In Europe and America art schools began to develop at about the same time, and these have made steady progress ever since. Silversmithing is not taught only as an academic subject: great emphasis is laid on the practical work. It is significant that a large proportion of the world output of silver objects in the present century has come from art schools and colleges: from Birmingham and Sheffield in England to the Konstfackskolan in Stockholm and the Cranbrook Academy of Art in the United States. From time to time exhibitions of the students' work are held, at which the objects are offered for sale; this gives the discerning collector the opportunity to acquire at a reasonable cost works which offer a good prospect of appreciating in value, especially since the unknown student of today may turn out to be one of the great artist-craftsmen of tomorrow.

Because of the system of hallmarking, prevalent not only in the United Kingdom but nowadays in most parts of the world, it is possible not only to date a piece of silver fairly accurately but also to identify its manufacturer. Even silver imported from abroad into Britain must be examined by an assay office and appropriately hallmarked. This age-old practice of 'signed' silver items is a good thing in many ways, not the least being the protection which it affords the customer; but in one respect it has created a somewhat artificial demand for the work of certain craftsmen. In antique silver the fact that a piece can be assigned to Paul de Lamerie, Paul Storr or Hester Bateman automatically boosts its market value, irrespective of aesthetic or antiquarian interest: this deplorable tendency has been fostered by the trade in general and by some sections of the press in particular. Paul de Lamerie, like anyone else, had his off days, and much of the latest work by Paul Storr is as hideously over-ornamented as the worst of Victorian silver (though it is perhaps more skilfully contrived). Fortunately modern silver is relatively free from this habit of fixing a price tag on an article according to the craftsman who made it. There are, however, a few exceptions: their names are particularly fashionable, and in fairness to the reader I must mention them and discuss their work. I do so not in the hope that the work of these silversmiths will be followed slavishly but because they have produced items which, both technically and artistically, are worthwhile. The silversmith of the modern period is too close to the present day for his reputation to have been built up artificially, as has been the case with many of the antique smiths, and such status as he may possess is more likely to have been won on merit and not so much on that nebulous quality of 'genius', with which some writers and publicists glibly explain away the current market value of the great names in the antique world.

The vicissitudes which the world silver industry has suffered in the present century have meant that the commercial side of it has undergone considerable contraction. Although the position has improved greatly in the past decade, it was feared at one time that silversmithing was a dying art. The rise of cheaper substitutes such as electroplate and stainless steel led to a tremendous falling-off in the demand for fine silver. The industry faced this problem partly by diversifying and embracing new techniques appropriate to these new materials, and partly by mergers and amalgamations of old-established businesses. Thus, in the United Kingdom today British Silverware Ltd includes such famous names as Adie Brothers, J.W. Benson, Garrard, Elkington, Mappin & Webb and Walker & Hall. Although the component companies continue to operate under their own name, the advantages of belonging to such an enormous manufacturing and retail group are obvious. This is not a new process in the silver industry but is one which has been evolving continually since the eighteenth century. Thus Storr and Mortimer, one of the most famous of the Regency firms, were merged with Hunt and Roskell in the 1840s, and they, in turn, amalgamated with Alfred Benson and Henry Webb in 1889, eight years later absorbing the more recently established firm of J.W. Benson, whose name was adopted by the group. Benson's merged with the other leading silver companies in 1963 to form British Silverware Ltd. In the same way Garrard's can trace their development from George Wickes, the goldsmith to King George I in 1721. The firm was acquired in 1952 by the Goldsmiths and Silversmiths Company (founded 1890), but the older-established and better known name of Garrard was retained as the designation of the new company. Although silversmithing is a craft which has often run in families (the Batemans, Hennells and Hemings are famous examples of this), very few of the older-established firms in existence today still have a personal link with the family of the founder (Spink's of London, though they have been a family firm for more than three centuries, have drifted away from their original role as silversmiths and, while continuing to produce medals and regalia, are today mainly involved in art and antique dealing). Edward Barnard & Sons of London take their name from Edward Barnard, foreman to Thomas Chainer, who took over the running of the business in the 1780s.

In the same way the personal element is not so strong today in the craftsmanship of fine silver (although there are many excellent designers, silversmiths and engravers operating on a freelance basis). The silversmith's establishment at the beginning of the nineteenth century was still a small affair comprising the smith himself and his apprentices. Articles were supplied direct from the craftsman to the consumer. The transformation of silversmithing—like furniture-making—from a craft into an industry, the introduction of mechanization in production and the development of wholesale and retail elements all served to destroy the personal character of silver and help to explain why there are relatively few outstanding names in modern silver. A few of the more important names are discussed below, but it should be stressed that objects bearing these names, or their initials, may range from an article designed and entirely made and finished by hand in the workshop of an artist-craftsman to the product of one of the large manufacturing and retail companies, involving many anonymous workers in the process. I can only say that, in deciding what is worthwhile in modern silver, one should consider the important criteria of quality, condition, rarity or exclusiveness and the elusive problem of taste. To this I would add an important rider—above all else it should appeal to you. As your experience of fine silver grows, your appreciation of its beauty will increase and, almost instinctively, you will be able to distinguish the top quality from the second-rate. The name applied to a particular piece should then be of secondary importance.

Asprey & Company of London ranks high among the retail fine arts dealers of the present day. Although the company can trace its history back to William Asprey in 1781, the turning-point came in the 1830s when premises were opened in Bond Street. Although now primarily concerned with jewelry, Asprey's still produce excellent silverware.

Barker Brothers ranked as one of the largest enterprises of the nineteenth century engaged in the manufacture of electroplate, and were the only British silversmiths ever to open a showroom in the United States (where it still exists, in New York). Despite the fact that the main business of this company has been in electroplate, some fine pieces of silverware have been produced during the past century.

Edward Barnard & Sons is carrying on the tradition of fine ornamental silver established by the great silversmith Anthony Nelme, who founded the business in 1689. The Barnards have been closely connected with the firm for 200 years. Many of the imposing presentation pieces of the Victorian era were produced by Barnards, and to this day the company continues to specialize in centrepieces and ornamental wares.

Black, Starr & Frost have the distinction of being one of the oldest surviving companies in New York. Founded in 1810 by Isaac Marquand, the firm has undergone many changes of name and partnership, the present title dating from 1876. Under the name of Ball, Black & Co. this firm was renowned in the middle of the last century for its ornate presentation items commemorating the Mexican War, the transatlantic cable and transatlantic shipping of the period. They manufactured and sold items ranging from hardware to jewelry, but in more recent years the original function of silversmithing has been emphasized in attractive modern silver, both ornamental and useful wares.

W.A. Bolin, the Swedish royal jewelers, present the curious and romantic story of a family business originally engaged in shipbuilding which eventually went into silversmithing. The shipbuilding enterprise in Gothenburg came to a sudden end with the deaths by drowning of John Bolin and his eldest son in 1836. A younger son, Charles, emigrated to Russia, married the daughter of the court jeweler in St Petersburg and entered the business himself. With his brother Henrik he built up a remarkable industry. Henrik's grandson was William A. Bolin, after whom the present Swedish company is named. A branch of the Russian business was established in Stockholm in 1916—barely a year before the Bolshevik Revolution resulted in the wholesale looting of the parent company and its untimely end. In addition to supplying the Tsars, Bolin's executed orders for many of the royal families of Europe, and the Swedish branch was automatically given the royal appointment on its foundation in 1916. A legacy of the Revolution was the number of Russian émigré craftsmen and designers who have worked at Bolin's of Stockholm in the last fifty years; but, especially since the Second World War, the rising generation of young Swedish designers have made their influence felt in the graceful pieces produced by this company. Bolin's probably have the highest reputation of all twentieth-century silversmiths.

As. Bonebakker, the Dutch royal jewelers, is another old-established family business, having been engaged in silversmithing in Amsterdam since 1792. Its elegant premises on Amsterdam's famous Rokin are noted for their choice, though relatively small, output of fine jewelry and silverware.

J.E. Caldwell, founded in Philadelphia in the late 1830s, is now one of the largest jewelers and silversmiths in the United States. Although the current trend has been away from the production of silver articles to a marked concentration on jewelry, Caldwell's nevertheless continue to produce fine tableware and occasional commissions of testimonial and presentation pieces.

L'Orfèvrerie Christophle, founded in 1839 by Charles Christophle, specializes in the manufacture of high-class electroplate. Christophle initiated the famous 'Baguette' pattern used in flatware (cutlery), and literally millions of these pieces must have been produced by this company since 1861. In 1951 Christophle's absorbed another famous French company, Cardeilhac, and now have branches in Switzerland, Italy, the United States and Argentina, catering for the international silver market.

Willliam Comyns & Sons of London is a good example of a comparatively small British company which specializes in the production of hand-made silverware. Perhaps because of the smallness of the firm and the select nature of its business, it was able to weather the post-war depression in the silver industry better than many others, but Comyns have made enormous progress in recent years, their average weekly turnover now exceeding the total for the whole of 1950.

James Dixon & Sons of Sheffield, founded in 1806, originally made a name for themselves in the production of Sheffield plate and Britannia wares, but over the years have produced some fine silver.

Elkington is one of those great household names in the silver industry, having revolutionized it in the middle of the nineteenth century with the invention of electroplating. Although some excellent silver has been sold under the name of this company, its fortune was largely made by electroplate in both its ornamental and industrial applications. Elkington's merged with Mappin & Webb in January 1963 to form British Silverware, and subsequently took over several other leading firms in the industry. It is a sad commentary on these times that Elkington's closed down in 1967 and no longer exist as a separate entity, though the Elkington brand name has appeared on goods manufactured by other members of the British Silverware group.

Fabergé is unkindly remembered today as the confectioner in precious metals who produced elegant trivia for the Imperial Court of Russia. But, apart from the celebrated Easter eggs and intricate *objets de vertu*, Fabergé deserves to be remembered for his uncompromising loyalty to the best of eighteenth-century traditions in design and craftsmanship at a time when the wealthier classes of Europe were suffering that curious nervous breakdown in taste which characterized the latter part of the nineteenth century. The company was formed in St Petersburg in 1842 by Gustave Fabergé, a French silversmith and jeweler, and given its distinctive character by his son, Peter Carl Fabergé, who, with his brother Agathon, personally supervised the design and production of the major portion of the Fabergé output. The company came to an abrupt end in 1917 with the Revolution in Russia, otherwise it might have developed in the way that its rival, Bolin's, did in Sweden. As it is, Fabergé is today a name to be conjured with and is one of the few (perhaps the only) names which the layman would instantly recognize. It is interesting to note that Fabergé had a legal battle in Britain in 1910 with the Worshipful Company of Goldsmiths, the Russian company contending that its products should be exempt from assay and hallmarking as works of art. Fabergé lost the case, and it is ironic to think that, in view of the fact that a great deal of fake Fabergé work is now on the market, the company's wares might have been better protected had more of it been hallmarked sixty years ago. The distinctive, rather decadent appearance of Fabergé trinkets has a great appeal for the modern collector, but this same distinctive appearance has led to the production of extremely dangerous forgeries. When one is paying so very much for the name it is advisable to purchase Fabergé items only from reputable dealers.

Garrard's of London have been the British crown jewelers since 1843 and have been responsible for some of the best silver in the British and other royal households in the past century. Although they are probably best known for their regimental silver and presentation items, Garrard's have produced much elegant silver in the modern streamlined idiom. In 1952 they amalgamated with the *Goldsmiths and Silversmiths Company*, Garrard's name being retained. The latter firm, founded in 1890, are best remembered for their 'Cherub' presentation series, pioneered by Charles and Richard Comyns, whom they took over in the early 1900s. Their chief designer, Alex Styles, has been responsible for many important items under the Garrard mark in recent years.

Hamilton & Inches is one of the few outstanding Scottish silversmiths of modern times. Founded in 1866 as a jewelry firm, they expanded into the production of silverware in the 1880s, and since then have built up a reputation for fine Scottish silver in traditional patterns.

The International Silver Company was an early American example of the kind of amalgamations which have taken place in Britain in recent years. Founded in 1898, it was renowned in pre-First World War days for its Britannia ware (not to be confused with antique silver of the Britannia standard). While the bulk of its business today is derived from contracts to supply cutlery and electroplate to catering organizations, hotels and airlines, it still produces some fine objects in sterling silver.

Georg Jensen of Denmark has the distinction of being the only silversmith in the world to be commemorated by a postage stamp, this philatelic honour being accorded to him in 1966 on the centenary of his birth. Jensen ranks as one of the greatest exponents of hand-made silver in an era when mechanization and mediocrity were all too apparent. Since 1904 the *atelier* which Jensen founded in Copenhagen has led the movement for modern silver of a superlative quality.

Liberty's of London, founded in 1875, were one of the first companies to embrace Art Nouveau and, indeed, this art form is known in Italy as 'Stile Liberty' to this day. Although better known for their furniture and textile designs, Liberty's have produced some good silver, that most sought after today being the famous Cymric range initiated at the turn of the century and produced as late as the 1920s. After many years of neglect Cymric silver has begun to attract the attention of collectors once more, and prices for this distinctive Art Nouveau style are now rising rapidly.

Mappin & Webb, now part of British Silverware, originated in Sheffield, specializing in cutlery. Over the past seventy years, however, they have been responsible for much excellent silverware, tea and coffee services and ornamental pieces.

Jean Puiforcat, 'the creator of modern silver', dominated the world of silver production in the 1920s, having pioneered the austere functional lines of 'Art Deco', the successor to Art Nouveau. Puiforcat, born in France in 1897, is still too near to our own time for his work to have taken its proper place in the development of silver over the past 100 years, and it has not yet recovered the fashionable position which it enjoyed before the Second World War. The propagandists who have been endeavouring to promote Art Deco as the collectable successor to Art Nouveau have brought Puiforcat into new prominence, and there are indications that the market has begun to respond.

Reed & Barton, an old-established Massachusetts silversmiths, have been mainly concerned in the production of electroplated goods for hotels, restaurants, etc. But over the past 140 years they have occasionally manufactured fine pieces in sterling silver, and these are now in great demand with American silver collectors.

Tiffany's of New York are mentioned in Chapter 3 in connection with the Art Nouveau glass pioneered by Louis Comfort Tiffany, but the company which his father founded and which survives to this day has also been highly successful in the manufacture and retail distribution of fine silverware. Not surprisingly the best known Tiffany silver is that associated with Art Nouveau, but both before and since that period it has produced silverware of a very high quality. Tiffany's, incidentally, were the first American company to adopt the British Sterling standard of 92·5 per cent fine silver, and while the silver of Louis Comfort Tiffany is almost in as great demand as his glass, it is the articles produced under the supervision of Edward Moore, chief silver designer of the company in the late nineteenth century, which today excite the greatest interest.

3 Glass

Although glass is one of the oldest man-made products, it is only within the past three centuries that its manufacture has become widespread and only within the past hundred years has its use been comparatively common. The earliest glass did not exist in a pure form but was applied to other substances as a glaze. Glazed stone beads dating from about 12,000 BC have been found in archaeological excavation in Mesopotamia. The oldest piece of pure glass dates from about 7000 BC and consists of small beads used as jewelry. The Egyptians were certainly manufacturing glass on a commercial scale by 2000 BC, but purely for personal adornment. A primitive form of pressed glass was evolved by 1200 BC, and small jars and containers for ointments began to appear about this time. Not until the intervention of glass-blowing in the century before the Christian era was the production of large vessels feasible. At about the same time the first relatively clear, transparent glass was discovered. The Greeks and the Romans brought glass manufacture to a fine art—the Portland Vase is an excellent example, thought to have been produced at Alexandria by Greek glassworkers about AD 50. Window glass began to appear in the third century, and about the same time millefiori patterns and glass mosaics were devised. Their significance is treated in some detail in the chapter on paperweights.

After the collapse of the Roman Empire glass manufacture died out in western Europe. Its traditions, however, were maintained by the Byzantine rulers at Constantinople, whence the art was probably brought to Venice in the eleventh century. The glass manufactured on the Venetian island of Murano was purely functional, but from the beginning of the Renaissance onwards (*c.* 1450) ornamental wares were increasingly produced. Much so-called Venetian glass of the sixteenth century was, in fact, made in other parts of Italy, and simultaneously the manufacture of fine glassware spread to the Low Countries, France, Germany, Spain

54

and England. We are not here concerned with the development of glassware in the 'antique' period, nor with the many different forms which it took. Suffice it to say that, from the time when George Ravenscroft invented his famous flint glass in 1675 right down to the present day, Britain has played a leading role, both technically and artistically, in this field. Compared with other antiques, English glass of the eighteenth century and Regency period is comparatively underrated and underpriced, so there is obviously plenty of scope for the shrewd collector of fairly modest means.

CUT GLASS

During the eighteenth and early nineteenth centuries successive governments had sought to raise revenue by various taxes on glass, and the methods by which this complicated excise was applied to the industry had considerable influence not only on the weight or thickness of glass but also on the type of glass used. With the removal of the glass excise in 1845 the industry was freed from restriction, and from this date the modern glass industry of Britain may be said to commence. One of the immediate results of the repeal of the excise was a renewed interest in cut glass. This form of decoration had been popular in the 1820s and 1830s, but went into decline for a short period. After 1845, when there were no restrictions on the use of thick glass, the fashion for deep-cutting revived and reached considerable proportions. Deep and elaborate cutting enjoyed a brief popularity around the middle of the century, epitomized perhaps by the huge glass fountain which F. and C. Osler of Birmingham designed as a centrepiece for the Great Exhibition of 1851. In a sense, however, this *chef d'œuvre* was a swan song, and though cut glass appears in succeeding years, it was never so elaborate again. The glass manufacturers delighted in displaying their technical skill in cutting deeply and profusely. The resulting article emitted a blaze of prismatic light, but the surface was rough and unpleasant to handle. In 1853 John Ruskin, in *Stones of Venice*, wrote, '. . . all cut glass is barbaric . . .'

While Ruskin was not the only writer of note to make a slashing condemnation of this form of glass, he gets all the blame, according to the *Encyclopaedia Britannica*, for bringing 'the craft into discredit and undoubtedly injuring the national glass trade'. It should be pointed out that the relative unpopularity of cut glass in the third quarter of the last century was more or less universal and can be attributed more to the rise of a cheap imitation in the shape of pressed glass. When it did return to favour, in the last decades of

55

the century, the cutting was carried out with greater precision and intricacy, the craftsmen being materially aided by the development of equipment capable of cutting complicated geometric patterns in a small space. The 1890s and the early years of this century were a period in which brilliant cut glass, as it was known, reached the acme of perfection. It is seen at its best in such articles as decanters, scent bottles, fruit bowls, jugs and cake baskets.

FANCY GLASS

Coloured and opaque glass were produced to some extent in the late eighteenth and early nineteenth centuries, and the so-called Nailsea and Bristol glassware of the 1800s is very well known to antique collectors. Fancy glass was in eclipse for most of the century, but in the 1870s and 1880s it enjoyed a widespread revival and was popular in both Europe and America. The earlier wares produced in this period were consciously derived from classical Venetian models, or embodied elements which were thought to have Venetian characteristics. Within a few years, however, glassmakers had progressed towards distinctive styles, colouring and materials which had never appeared before. In the restless search for novelty the manufacturers produced some very odd and unusual kinds of glass, using techniques which were applied over a relatively brief period. Some of these styles and types of glass were extremely important during the time when they were current, and rank among the most desirable today, as far as the collector is concerned. Because of their importance I have dealt with them individually.

Others made little impact and had only passing interest for the collector at the time of their manufacture, although nowadays the market in fancy glass is rising steadily and the more gimmicky varieties are finding ready purchasers. Unlike all silver (which is hallmarked) and most porcelain, glass seldom bears the name, imprint or trademark of its manufacturer. One can sometimes establish with certainty the maker of a particular object because of the material used or the style of decoration, which happened to be peculiar to that particular producer, but in the majority of cases this is impossible, since there was always a great deal of imitation in the glass industry. This is not to decry the imitations, which might be—and often were—superior to the original, but it must be emphasized that few companies had a monopoly of any given styles, and therefore to classify articles according to their factories would be pointless. For this reason collectors usually confine their interest to certain types of glass rather than attempting to collect the wares of one or more manufacturers. The antique glass collector may concentrate on Nailsea, but it is unlikely that more than a small percentage of the blue glass he acquires actually emanated from the glassworks of that village.

Among the many kinds of fancy glass which are now beginning to attract the attention of the collector is Amberina, a clear yellow glass shading almost imperceptibly into red at the top. Reverse Amberina is, as one would expect, a delicate red colour shading into yellow at the top. This effect was achieved by the judicious refining of certain portions of an amber-coloured glass till the desired reddish effect was achieved. Given the right amount of time, patience and heat, it was sometimes possible to achieve an attractive purple shading. This fuchsia Amberina is comparatively rare and highly prized by collectors. Amberina was widely produced in the last two decades of the nineteenth century, and other colours, such as green or blue, may be found in combination with the amber or fuchsia. Although it was produced in Europe as well as America, the chief exponents of Amberina were the New England Glass Company of Cambridge, Massachusetts, and the Libbey Glass Company of Toledo, Ohio, which succeeded it. A few pieces by the former company were marked with its initials in a rectangle, while the latter etched its name on a relatively large number of pieces. Marked Amberina is eagerly sought out by collectors, but unmarked items may be just as desirable, or more so, on account of their colour or shape. A rare and short-lived variant of this kind of glass was termed Plated Amberina, a speciality of the New England Glass Company in the late 1880s. It is easily identified by its opaque lining, often with a bluish tinge, and—more importantly—by the presence of vertical ribbing on the outer layer. It is the latter characteristic which distinguishes it from the famous Peach Blow glass manufactured by Hobbs, Brockunier and Company at Wheeling, West Virginia.

Peach Blow is the name given to several types of fancy glass produced in the United States from 1886 onwards. The name is a slight corruption of Peach Bloom, the description given to a rare Chinese porcelain vase which fetched the unprecedented sum of $18,000 when auctioned earlier that year when the estate of the late Mrs Mary Morgan was disposed of. Its delicate beauty and great rarity inspired several manufacturers to produce fancy glass in imitation of it, with varying success. Both the New England and the Mt Washington companies produced a single-layered glass under this name, easily distinguishable from each other on account of the colours used. The best known of the Peach Blow glasses, however, was that produced by Hobbs Brockunier, and this took the form of a double-layered or lined glass. The outer layer shades, like Amberina, from a rich tawny to a deep red and has a creamy opal lining. Appropriately enough, the most famous products in Wheeling Peach Blow were simply replicas of the celebrated Morgan Vase. Thomas Webb & Sons and Stevens & Williams of Stourbridge also produced layered varieties of Peach Blow, but the English types are comparatively scarce and priced accordingly.

Another interesting, and increasingly popular, type of glass is that known as Mother of Pearl (often abbreviated to M.O.P.), usually characterized by a nacreous lustre on the outer surface. It consists of two or more layers with a pattern showing through to the outside of the piece. The patterns, produced by internal air traps, were pressed into various designs such as Moiré and Diamond Quilted, Raindrop and Peacock Eye. Other variants of M.O.P. are Satin and Rainbow Mother of Pearl, and these were extremely popular with glassmakers on both sides of the Atlantic. Mother of Pearl glassware is fairly plentiful, but its popularity with collectors is such that the market for it is rising steadily.

The New England Glass Company of New Bedford, Massachusetts, specialized in a number of attractive types of fancy glass: they included Agata (1885), Pomona (1885) and Green Opaque (1887). Agata glass was characterized by a metallic stain giving a spider's web effect. Pomona also bore a metallic stain round the upper border of the object, with transparent coloured metallic stains forming attractive floral designs on the main body of the piece. Students of fancy glass distinguished between 'first grind' and 'second grind' Pomona. In the former, the glass was coated with an acid resistant substance which was then intricately carved. When the object was dipped into acid the glass was etched where the 'resist' had been cut into. The resulting surface of finely etched lines has a brilliant quality which rightly endears it to the collector. 'Second grind' Pomona had the acid resistant substance applied mechanically and the etched glass was given a speckled appearance which lacks something of the brilliance of 'first grind' Pomona. Green Opaque derives its name from its appearance. Decoration was effected by applying a blue mottled stain to the upper portion of the object, and a narrow gold border was added to accentuate the lower part of the mottling.

The Mount Washington Glass Company specialized in a curious kind of glass known as Royal Flemish, first manufactured about 1890. Its principal distinguishing feature was its finely painted enamels with designs in high relief. The commonest motifs were classical medallions, but winged subjects (birds, cherubs and mythical creatures) were also depicted.

Other companies which produced their own distinctive glass included C.F. Monroe of Meriden, Connecticut, whose Wave Crest, Nakara and Kelva glass were popular around the beginning of the present century. Smith Brothers of New Bedford were noted for their beautiful glass lampshades, produced from about 1880 onwards. The Union Glass Company of Somerville, Massachusetts, manufactured a type of fancy glass known as Kew Blas (an anagram of W.S. Blake, the factory manager) which was also used for lampshades. On the other side of the Atlantic the principal British manufacturers of fancy glass were Webb and Sons and Stevens & Williams. The latter company, at Brierley Hill in Staffordshire, produced many of the types of fancy glass already mentioned. In addition, however, they specialized in a two-layered glass containing a sandwich filling of thin silver foil. This type of glass, known as Silveria, appeared in the early years of this century and is now highly esteemed by the discerning collector. Both these companies manufactured an unusual three-coloured glass known as Alexandrite. Basically amber, the glass was reheated in such a way as to produce fuchsia and blue shades at the extremities. Produced at the turn of the century, this glass is thought to have been peculiar to these two firms and is greatly prized nowadays. It should not be confused with a Bohemian glass of about the same period which is found with the word 'Alexandrite' stamped on the base. This was a single-coloured (usually amethyst) glass produced by the renowned artist Koloman Moser.

To a limited extent fancy glass was also produced on the Continent of Europe. The wares of the great French glass-houses, Gallé, Lalique and Daum, are noted below, as are those of the leading Bohemian manufacturers. The leading American exponents of art glass, such as Heisey, Tiffany and Webb, are also dealt with. The vogue for fancy glass was strongest in the United States, and nowadays the revival of interest in this field is centred there. The prolific literature on the subject, from general works such as Patrick Darr's *Guide to Art and Pattern Glass* and *Art Nouveau Glass* by Ray and Lee Grover, to specialized monographs on Steuben and Tiffany, is predominantly American, and there is little chance now of the collector in the United States making a lucky find. In Britain the situation is still fluid, and fine and rare examples of Burmese ware have even been known to turn up in church bazaars and scout jumble sales priced at a modest shilling or two.

The year 1886 was a memorable one in the British glass industry, since it marked the debut of the fairy light and a type of fancy glass known as Burmese ware. The two events were unrelated in their origins, but combined in the business enterprises of the two companies which held the respective patents, they had a formidable, if brief, impact on the fashionable world of the late nineteenth century. The fairy light evolved from a simple night light which was patented by George Clarke as early as 1844. Samuel Clarke developed the idea further, and in 1857 patented a high-grade wax light which was capable of burning for up to twelve hours.

The fairy light was the ornamental counterpart of the nursery night light, and seems to have been first produced early in 1886. The wax lights were enclosed ingeniously in glass bulbs of delicate hues, and they could be adapted for a variety of purposes. They were used as bracket lights or hung in large clusters to form chandeliers or, as they are best remembered, hung from slender chains in gardens and conservatories to illuminate the flower beds and accentuate the beauty of the plants.

A contemporary account described fairy lights transformed into centrepieces for the dining table:

'They are small lights, which are placed in the centre of a circular flower vase and each is covered with a tinted glass shade, some opal, some pale rose, some of the tenderest of soft green. The flower circle was filled with moss and ferns, with just two or three pink and yellow tulip buds in each. The softness of the light gave an added beauty to the flowers and ferns, and as the fairy lamps are quite low on the table, the effect was extremely becoming to the diners. . . .'

The lights were known variously as the 'Fairy', the 'Fairy-Pyramid' and the 'Wee Fairy' in descending order of size. Appropriately enough, the trademark showed a fairy, and this is usually found stamped on the base of the wax light container. The earliest, and most highly prized, examples show the fairy with her left hand close to her head. Late examples, dating around the turn of the century, are stamped with the trade name 'Cricklight', an allusion to the company's factory in Cricklewood, North London. Fairy lights were marketed by Clarks at prices varying from six shillings a dozen for those with clear glass to thirty-six shillings a dozen for 'Cameo shades'. A wide variety of styles and shades of glass was used, in a futile effort to keep one jump ahead of business rivals, for the popularity accorded to the fairy light soon induced other manufacturers to imitate it.

Second only to the Cameo shades in expensiveness, but by far the most popular with collectors today, was the attractive form of glass known as Burmese ware, which, in spite of its name, originated in the United States. This exquisitely blended glass, with its semi-opaque salmon pink colour, shading imperceptibly into delicate hues of yellow, was discovered and patented by the Mount Washington Glass Company of New Bedford, Massachusetts, in December 1885. The English rights were acquired by Thomas Wilkes Webb, one of the most astute glass manufacturers in the Midlands. He had begun producing articles of a decorative nature in iridescent glass a decade earlier and won the Grand Prix at the Paris Exhibition of 1878 with his 'Bronze' glass. Other glass for which the firm of Thomas Webb and Sons was famous included 'Peach', 'Old Roman' and 'Tricolor', but it was the superb 'Burmese' which made Webb a household name in the late 1880s.

Clarke did not himself manufacture the glass bulbs for his fairy lights, and at first commissioned Stuart and Sons of Stourbridge to carry out this part of the work. When Webb's Burmese glass appeared in September 1886 Clarke was captivated by the radiant qualities of this material, and from the beginning of 1887 onwards fairy lights, chandeliers, bracket lamps and candelabra were produced for Clarke by Webb in Burmese ware. Although costly, Burmese ware, because of its almost magical appearance, endured in popularity far longer than most of the other fancy glass produced by Webb. As late as November 1890 the *Pottery Gazette* was commenting that Burmese ware was still a favourite. Since it was so popular with Queen Victoria during her Golden Jubilee, Webbs were allowed to call it Queen's Burmese Ware.

The increasing use of electric light towards the end of the century marked the demise of Clarke's ornamental fairy light, and fancy glass such as Burmese ware was not in sympathy with the harsh qualities of artificial light. Nowadays, of course, the fairy lights and table lamps of eighty years ago are eminently collectable, even the smallest and least significant costing at least a pound or two. At the other end of the scale, lamps in Burmese ware are exceedingly costly. A night-light stand in this material made £350 ($840) at Sotheby's in October 1966.

TIFFANY GLASS

Louis Comfort Tiffany (1848–1933) is aptly described by his biographer, Robert Koch, as 'a rebel in glass', for he did more

61

than any one man to revolutionize the art glass of the late nineteenth and early twentieth centuries. A member of the famous Tiffany family (which is a household name in America to this day in the fields of modern applied art and the material aspects of gracious living), he originally trained as a painter. In 1876, however, he was greatly inspired by the decorative arts of the Far East, exhibited at the Philadelphia Centennial Exhibition. He experimented with coloured glass and in 1878 established a glass factory in New York, specializing in the production of fancy glass for stained-glass windows. This enterprise failed when his premises were burned down. With the scraps of coloured glass left over from this venture he began to turn his attention to jewelry and floral decoration for mounting on boxes and vessels of blown glass. During the next decade he progressed slowly towards his ideal, and in 1893 inaugurated the Tiffany Furnaces at Corona, Long Island. The products of this factory were exhibited at the Columbian Exposition that year and were hailed as an immediate success. For forty years, until his death, Tiffany produced art glass in the numerous different styles which were appropriate to the period, spanning the years from Art Nouveau to Art Deco. By the beginning of the century Tiffany glass was already considered eminently collectable and, though the company was in production as late as 1936, and its output was vast, such is the magic of the name that even the later Tiffany wares are highly prized today, barely forty years after their appearance.

The character of Tiffany glass is quite bewildering in its complexity. A sort of restlessness seemed to have overtaken him, as the catalogue of the 1900 Paris Exposition commented, '. . . in common with most artistic natures . . . Mr Tiffany loses much of his interest in an achievement as soon as it deserves that name'. His peacock feathers and large foliate patterns, somewhat redolent of Japanese art, were the essence of Art Nouveau, and with the latter's recent return to popularity, Tiffany glass has been given an added boost. Tiffany continued to produce blown glass in this faintly decadent style for many years after it had generally gone out of fashion. Nevertheless, the later products of his factory also included an appreciable amount of engraved and cameo glass, not to mention useful wares such as lamps and lampshades. It should be noted, however, that Tiffany was not without his imitators and, in particular, his famous iridescent glass, patented as early as 1880, was copied by glass manufacturers in America and Europe. The collector need not worry unduly about the correct attribution of early twentieth-century iridescent glass, since quality, rather than the name of the company, is the important factor in determining its value. Some excellent glass, in the manner of Tiffany iridescent glass, was produced by the Bohemian glass-houses, especially J. Lötz Witwe of Klostermühle, whose wares are keenly appreciated nowadays by Continental collectors.

GALLÉ GLASS

If Louis Tiffany bent the styles of Art Nouveau to his own will, Emile Gallé (1846–1904) was the more original genius in creating the style of his day. Like Tiffany, he came from a family already interested in modern applied art, his father, Charles Gallé, had produced ceramics, glassware and furniture. Young Gallé learned the glass trade at Meisenthal in Germany, and by 1865 was designing fine crystal ware for production in the family glass factory at Nancy. Two years later he founded his own workshop for decorative glassware, and by the mid-1870s art glass from the Gallé factory was earning a reputation for its fine craftsmanship. Gallé's own reputation as an artist in this difficult medium was established by the Paris Exposition of 1878 with the range and versatility of his opaline glass, marble glass and treble-layered glass encasing gold leaf between the layers. The expositions of 1884 and 1889 served only to enhance still further his reputation for inventiveness and originality. He drew extensively on the art of medieval Europe and the art of Japan which, since the opening of that country to Westerners in 1853, had become increasingly popular in America and Europe. It is certainly true to say that 'Japonisme' had a decisive effect on Gallé from 1889 onwards, and this was epitomized in his so-called 'nature style'. He used floral motifs to a large extent in decorating his glassware, and his intimate knowledge of horticulture is demonstrated in the accuracy of the modelling.

Much of his glassware was inscribed with lines of poetry—the *verreries parlantes*; all of it was redolent of the poetic style of Art Nouveau. Undoubtedly Gallé reached the zenith of his success in 1889. He opened a decorators' studio in that year in order to cope with the tremendous demand for his glassware, and from then onwards the inventiveness and originality with which he had imbued his work became less and less evident. After his death the Gallé factory continued to produce fine glassware in similar styles as late as the 1920s at least, but it was a mere shadow of its former self, and little seems to have been recorded of the firm in its declining years. Gallé's works were lauded uncritically in his lifetime, but despised and neglected after his death. Since the Second World War, however, there has been a reassessment of Gallé and his glassware, and it is again attracting the attention of the serious collector. The output of the Gallé factory was large and astonishingly varied—seldom are two identical pieces found. The best glass was produced between 1880 and 1890, while the most prolific period was from 1890 to 1904; most of the collectable Gallé wares were manufactured in those twenty-four years. An interesting point to note is that after 1889 Gallé glass was signed, and this is an invaluable aid to the collector. Prior to that date, few pieces of glass were signed, and it is significant that glassmakers everywhere began to adopt this practice from this time onward.

OTHER FRENCH MANUFACTURERS

While Gallé is still the chief name in modern French glassware, there are many others whose products were, and are, of interest to the collector. Chief among them were the Daum family of Nancy, who continued the tradition and styles initiated by Gallé. During the 1920s and 1930s René Lalique (1860–1945) dominated the French glass industry, specializing in table glass—vases, goblets, jars and bowls—decorated with moulded relief ornaments on a frosted background. Lalique automated his production far more than the Daums, and for this reason much of his glassware (especially moulded and pressed glass) is not so highly regarded by collectors. One form of Lalique glass which is now eagerly collected is the scent bottle. For many years Lalique supplied the great parfumier, Coty, with exquisitely shaped bottles, and other manufacturers of perfume were not slow to follow suit. Not so long ago these bottles would have been discarded, or would have changed hands for a shilling or two at most. Nowadays, however, they can be worth up to several pounds.

MODERN EUROPEAN GLASS

The manufacture of fine collectable glass has spread evenly all over Western Europe, from Spain and Italy to Scandinavia. For example, the Functionalist designs of the Swedes Simon Gate and Edward Hald were extremely popular in Scandinavia before the Second World War, and their taste and innate good sense are now commending their glassware to the world at large. Similar styles were adopted in Denmark by Jacob Bang and in Norway by Sverre Petterson, and today Scandinavian glassware, with its simple clean lines, is highly regarded as a symbol of graciousness without ostentation. While Finnish glassware tends to follow the same patterns, the plain, usually green, glass vases designed by

Alvar Aalto and produced at the glass factory of Karhola-Iittala in the past thirty years deserve special mention. The loose, asymmetrical rhythms and extreme technical simplicity of Aalto's glass created a sensation when it first appeared in 1938, and it is still regarded as strangely ahead of its time. From the collector's viewpoint this is the sort of glass which could suddenly rise in popularity in ten years' time or less and is certainly worth watching out for today.

In the Low Countries art glass was dominated in the early years of this century by Chris Lebeau. While much of his earlier work in the 1920s was an exaggerated harking back to Art Nouveau, with striking use of elongated shapes and iridescent surfaces, he also embraced the Functionalism which swept Scandinavia. Another Functionalist is Andries Copier, whose spherical flower vases have achieved international fame since they were first produced in 1928. Copier's early work consisted of the so-called 'Unica' pieces, elegant vases in fairly thin tinted glass with moulded ribbing.

In Czechoslovakia and Austria the traditions of the old Bohemian glassmakers are maintained. Glass production has been a nationalized industry in Czechoslovakia since 1948, but this has in no way diminished its quality or importance. Rather the opposite is true, since generous state aid is given to art schools and technical colleges to ensure that the up-and-coming designers and craftsmen have the best tuition. This has resulted in the foundation of the Creative Glass Centre in Prague in 1952 to foster good relations between the industry and artists and designers, and to encourage research into new techniques of decorating glassware. While Bohemian Crystal is still the most important product of the Czech factories, increasing interest is being shown in art glass as well as glass engraved with figures and floral ornament.

The old-established Bohemian firm of J. & L. Lobmeyr is now the leading glass company in Austria, its connections with its traditional home having been gradually severed since Czechoslovakia became independent in 1918. The outstanding products of this factory are enamelled glass and finely engraved glass. The success of Lobmeyrs in the art field was undoubtedly due to the genius of Wilhelm von Eiff, who was associated with the firm in the early 1920s. As professor of glass engraving at the Stuttgart technical school von Eiff has exerted a tremendous influence on glass-cutters and engravers not only in Austria and Czechoslovakia but throughout the world, during the past forty years.

In Italy, traditional birthplace of modern glassmaking, there was a revival of Venetian styles in the 1860s, and this has continued

E

down to the present day. The outstanding figures in modern Italian glass manufacture are Paolo Venini, whose firm began operating at Murano in 1921, and Ercole Barovier, who is at present art director of Barovier & Toso, also based on Murano. Much fine hand-made glass is available—at a price—from the modern Murano glass houses, and ranks high on the list of collectable mementoes of a trip to Italy.

STEUBEN GLASS

Art glass was manufactured in Steuben from 1903 onwards by L.G. Hawkes and Frederick Carder. Carder, born in Staffordshire in 1863, served his apprenticeship as a glassmaker with Stevens & Williams of Brierley Hill and emigrated to the United States in 1903. For thirty years the Steuben company (and the Corning Glass Company, which took it over in 1918) were under Carder's influence, and during this period he was responsible for the production of coloured glass—about sixty different colours in several thousand shades. Among his most famous creations were Verre de Soiz, a pearly, iridescent and slightly metallized glass, and Intarsia glass, distinguished by the solid objects trapped inside it.

Until fairly recently Steuben glass was generally quite cheap, but in the past few years it has soared enormously in value, and one would need a deep purse to form a reasonable collection of Aurene, Cluthra Ivrene and Rosaline glass. A good proportion of Steuben glass was not marked, though, to an expert, it presents little problem in identification. Marked pieces, bearing the Steuben imprint or Carder's name, are very much in demand and fetch the highest prices. Interest in Steuben is naturally strongest in America, but a large amount of it found its way across the Atlantic and it is worth watching out for.

HEISEY GLASS

Eminently collectable these days are the products of the Heisey Glass Company of Newark, Ohio, particularly the moulded glass animal figures in which this firm specialized in the early years of this century. Their attractive crystal horses, elephants, buffaloes and birds have been re-issued in recent years by the Imperial Glass Corporation of Bellaire, Ohio, which acquired the original moulds and production equipment of the Heisey organization in 1958. The re-issues may be identified by the Imperial 'IG' monogram found on the base of stemmed or footed articles and on the inside or bottom of bowls. The sinuous lines of Heisey wares in clear, coloured glass are seen at their best in the attractive bowls, vases, candlesticks and table ornaments, and the styles known as Fandango or Diamond Swag and Waverley are keenly sought by knowledgeable collectors.

ENGRAVED GLASS

Engraving, as opposed to deep-cutting, had been applied fitfully to glassware in Britain for several centuries, but it was not until the early nineteenth century that it became really popular. In the previous century engraved work had been employed in the production of the famous Jacobite glasses, portraying the Young Pretender and the symbolism of the lost cause, but little else that was in any way distinguished. Decorative motifs were engraved on the bowls of wine glasses in the early nineteenth century, but engraving was invariably subordinated to cutting and only used on difficult shapes or very thin glass where deep-cutting was impracticable. As the century progressed, however, increasing use was made of engraving on straight-sided goblets or vases, particularly for quasi-commemorative purposes. To this period, for example, belong the so-called Sunderland glasses, featuring the famous bridge across the Tyne. Although the bridge was actually opened in 1796, glassware commemorating this event was still being engraved as late as 1840. It seems surprising that the engravers should have found so little scope for their activities; apart from Sunderland Bridge and occasional 'neo-Jacobite' subjects, the most popular motifs were nautical—Nelson, Duncan, St Vincent and the scenes of their most famous naval battles.

When cut glass went into eclipse in the third quarter of the century, engraved glass came into its own, and it is significant to note that this type of glass dominated the British glassware stands at the international exhibitions in London (1862) and Paris (1867). Many of the engravers came to Britain from Bohemia, where the craft had flourished since the seventeenth century. They worked independently of the glass manufacturers in many instances and established important businesses in their own right. Among the best known of these were the engraving firms of John Millar in Edinburgh, Paul Oppity in London and Frederick Kay in Stourbridge.

Gradually the styles of engraving became more florid and sumptuous. In the 1880s 'rock crystal', in which the entire surface was polished to make it uniformly bright, became fashionable. At this point also the engraving tended to become deeper. The greatest exponents of rock crystal in the closing years of the century were

Thomas Webb & Sons, the engraving being carried out by Kay and William Fritsche, who operated independent workshops within the Webb factory. To a lesser extent Joseph Kelly produced engraved rock crystal for Stevens & Williams in the 1880s, and this company also pioneered intaglio work—a cross between deep-cutting and engraving (in that it consisted of deep engraving).

Distinct from, but related to, engraved work was the cameo glass which Webb and Stevens & Williams produced in the 1880s and 1890s. This consisted of glasswork decorated in high relief in the manner of the Portland Vase (a popular subject for imitation). The friezes were actually carved in the glass using variations of deep-cutting techniques, but most of the surrounding decoration was supplied by wheel-engraving in the usual manner. Apart from a few pieces of cameo glass made in the United States by immigrants from Stourbridge, this type of glassware was not produced outside Britain, and it is in that country that it is most appreciated nowadays.

Cameo glass, like deep-cut glass, has been subject to the vagaries of fashion over the years, but engraved glass has enjoyed a more lasting popularity, and this is demonstrated today when limited editions of engraved goblets, chalices and vases are quickly snapped up. The principal British companies today in this field are James Powell (Whitefriars), Webb Corbett, Stuart & Sons and Royal Brierley (formerly Stevens & Williams). They employ artists and designers of a very high calibre, such as Irene Stevens and David Hammond of Webb Corbett, Deane Meanley and Tom Jones at Royal Brierley and John Luxton of Stuart & Sons. Among the many freelance engravers whose work is highly prized and worth collecting as antiques of the future may be mentioned Laurence Whistler, Anthony Pope, Sheila Elmhirst, Stephen Rickard, Dorothy Brown and Harold Gordon.

Though the equipment used by the glass engraver has improved since the late eighteenth century—from the primitive stone wheel rotated by means of a foot treadle to powered lathes and modern abrasives—the individual designer and craftsman is as important as ever, and on his skill and dexterity depend the beauty and brilliance of the finished article. Only the finest materials are used in the production of full lead crystal, a mixture of silica and silver sand to which about 30 per cent lead is added to give it its brilliant lustre, strength and durability and that shimmering clarity which is so enhanced by hand-cutting and engraving, almost dazzling the eye with its myriads of dancing lights. Engraved crystal is produced for purely decorative effect, but it would seem that the best items to buy while current are those limited editions produced in commemoration of certain events. Among the outstanding pieces produced in recent years, for example are crystal goblets marking the quatercentenary of William Shakespeare, the Coronation of Queen Elizabeth in 1953 and the Investiture of the Prince of Wales in 1969. In addition, Royal Brierley produced an edition of 500 goblets showing a bust of Sir Winston Churchill and recording his birth, family crests, office as Prime Minister and his citizenship of the United States. This item retailed at thirty guineas ($76) and sold out shortly after it came on the market. Commemorative items are dealt with in greater detail in chapter 10.

4 Glass paperweights

The art of glass mosaics known as *millefiori* (literally 'a thousand flowers') was known to the Egyptians thousands of years ago, but it was the Venetians who adapted it in the time of the Renaissance to the glass curiosities known as paperweights. The technique of making these tiny glass mosaics was practised by the glassworkers on the island of Murano near Venice (where it is carried on to this day). When one considers the painstaking techniques required to draw out the minute strands of vari-coloured glass and mould them into hexagons and stars with the design preserved throughout (in much the same fashion that the name of a seaside resort appears in a stick of rock) one can begin to appreciate the amount of work involved in their production.

Short lengths of the bundles of cane were laid on a bed plate and formed into attractive patterns. Each bundle might contain anything from six to fifty canes, and up to a hundred bundles would comprise the set-up of a paperweight with an average diameter of three inches. Various motifs other than florets were often incorporated, featuring animals, insects or dancing figures. Although the scattered patterns were the most popular, other types of millefiori were produced which have a considerable charm. Venetian millefiori weights were certainly well established by the end of the fifteenth century. In his history of the Venetian Republic, *De Situ Venetae Orbis*, published about 1495, Marcantonio Sabellico speaks of 'a little ball including all the sorts of flowers which clothe the meadows in spring', among the products of the Murano glass-houses. Nevertheless, it appears that the manufacture of glass paperweights was conducted at Venice in a very sporadic fashion, and few of these Venetian weights have survived.

Something of a revival in the production of millefiori weights at Murano came in the middle of the nineteenth century, when Pierre Bigaglia began to make glass paperweights. The earliest known specimen of a Bigaglia weight incorporates canes bearing the date 1845 and the initials P.B. This particular weight was unusual in its cuboid shape, but others attributed to Bigaglia conform to the more usual spherical shape. Bigaglia displayed glass paperweights at the Exhibition of Austrian Industry held in May 1845 (it must be remembered that at that time Northern Italy formed the Austrian province of Lombardo-Venezia) and caught the attention of a M. Peligot of the Paris Chamber of Commerce. He was subsequently responsible for introducing the art to the French glass manufacturers, three of whom in particular became renowned for their fine paperweights. The principal factories were located at Baccarat and St Louis in the Vosges and at Clichy near Paris, where a glassworks was in existence from about 1840 till the Siege of Paris in 1870–1.

The esteem in which the glass paperweights of Baccarat, Clichy and St Louis are held is justified by their superlative workmanship, vivid colouring and exquisite designs. Yet the period in which these paperweights was produced was extremely short. At the very outside it extended for only five years, from 1845 to 1850, though from the existence of dated examples it may have been much shorter in the case of the individual factories. Dated and initialled weights are recorded, for example, from Baccarat between 1846 and 1849, from St Louis between 1845 and 1848, and from Clichy during 1849 and 1850. Two isolated examples are known from Baccarat with the dates 1853 and 1858, but both are thought to be unique, and it is agreed that the manufacture of paperweights by this factory was more or less abandoned by 1850. Not all French paperweights, by any means, were dated, and there is always a possibility that many of the undated examples which have been attributed to Baccarat, Clichy or St Louis on stylistic grounds were produced at some later date. Moreover, although many anonymous paperweights have been attributed with a reasonable degree of certainty to one or other of these three factories, there are other weights whose source of manufacture has not been identified, and some of the rarest and most unusual French paperweights may have been made in other glassworks. It should, perhaps, be emphasized that French glass paperweights were, at best, a sideline to the main business of the factories. This accounts for their relative scarcity and the loving care and exquisite craftsmanship lavished on them. Had they ever been produced on a commercial basis, it is extremely doubtful whether they would have exhibited the same high degree of skill and artistry. They were probably produced merely as attractive novelties and were sold for a few francs each at the most.

Although the scattered patterns were the most popular, other types of millefiori were used which have a considerable charm. Comparatively rare are the mushrooms, in which the central tufts of millefiori are surrounded by threads of opaque glass entwined in a latticed pattern (hence the term *latticinio*). Another of the rarer types is the overlay, consisting of a mushroom coated with white opaque glass and an overlay of colour. The millefiori centre could be viewed through 'windows' ground into the sides and top of the globe. Overlays, especially those of Clichy, rank among the most expensive of glass paperweights, and prices up to £1000 ($2400) or more have been paid for particularly fine ones. Millefiori may also be found arranged in a serpentine pattern; these 'snakes' were a speciality of the St Louis factory and are exceedingly scarce, being likely to fetch anything from £200 ($480) upwards when they turn up in the saleroom. Millefiori bouquets and garlands, as opposed to the scattered motifs, were favoured by both St Louis and Clichy and also command fairly high prices nowadays.

Distinct from the weights with a millefiori composition are those which incorporate flowers, insects or animals. In general, it is these paperweights decorated in patterns other than millefiori which command the higher prices. Among the more popular forms of paperweight is that which incorporates a bouquet or posy of flowers either on a plain opaque or coloured ground or set on an attractive latticed base. Each of the three factories had its own speciality in this field. Bouquet paperweights from Clichy, for example, invariably have a pink or blue ribbon tying the stalks. Both Baccarat and St Louis produced bouquets consisting of upstanding flowers. St Louis also produced a very rare weight showing a bouquet of flowers in a white spiral basket above which is a handle of pink ribbon enclosed by a white spiral twist. It is interesting to note some recent prices for bouquet weights, compared with the prices realized for similar items at various times in the past fifteen years. A fine Clichy bouquet on a *latticinio* ground, which made £210 in the sale of the Guggenheim collection in 1960, fetched ten times that sum (approx. $5000) at Sotheby's in May 1968. An attractive St Louis blue-ground flat bouquet weight made £800 ($1920) in the same sale; at Sotheby's in March 1957 it fetched £105 ($252) and eight years later went for £200 ($480).

Individual flower weights are also keenly prized by collectors. Among the many flowers which have been identified are bell-flowers, bluebells, clematis, crocuses, dahlias, pansies, periwinkles, poinsettia, primroses, fuchsias, roses, chrysanthemums and geraniums. Some flowers are comparatively plentiful; others are extremely rare, if not unique. Generally speaking, the flowers adopted were peculiar to one factory or, if used by more than one, can usually be identified by the technique or treatment employed. All three leading French factories, for example, produced paper-weights featuring dahlias, but in each case subtle differences may be noted which help to identify one from another. The Baccarat dahlias are found in a number of colours, blues, reds, mauve or yellow, usually with honeycomb or white star-dust centres, green leaves and stalk. They occur either in clear glass or inside a wreath of coloured canes. A very rare type, also from Baccarat, consisted of a large dahlia with four layers of deep red petals, white star-dust centre, surrounded by leaves and a very short stalk. The St Louis dahlias are also found in two distinct types: a small flower with large stalk and leaves and a large flower head more or less occupying the entire space. In the former type the flowers are mostly gentian blue, rose pink or yellow, with green leaves and stalk. Although they are sometimes found in clear glass, the main distinction of St Louis dahlias was their coloured or opaque grounds. White spiral grounds are also known and a rare and un-usual nacreous metallic ground surrounded by a red or pink and white spiral. The latter, showing a large dahlia head, has layers of striped petals surrounded by green leaves. The colours used were pale and deep pink, light and dark mauve, and yellow streaked with black, this last being very rare. The Clichy dahlias differ from the Baccarat types not only in the colours used but in their in-clusion of a peculiar cog-shaped central cane—a distinctive feature. These weights may be found in clear glass or on white *latticinio* or spiral bases.

Other flowers were only used by one factory. The only example so far recorded of a forget-me-not came from the St Louis glass-house. A rare, though not unique flower weight, which was peculiar to Clichy, shows a convolvulus or morning glory. This is a most unusual variety invariably found on a white spiral ground. An excellent specimen in the Applewhaite-Abbott collection made £90 ($216) at Sotheby's in February 1953; £480 ($1152) when it appeared there again twelve years later and then went for £2250 ($5300) in May 1968. A Clichy convolvulus bouquet weight made £5200 ($12,480) in 1966, a world record price. The humble daisy is the subject of two extremely rare paperweights: only one of each has been recorded from Baccarat and St Louis. The former was a pure white marguerite with a large honeycomb centre, while the other had thirteen white and pink elongated petals with a curious yellow rosette cane in the centre.

Flower weights which also include a bird or an insect are relatively uncommon and because of this are in great demand.

The most popular type shows a butterfly hovering over a flower (Baccarat or St Louis), but others recorded show caterpillars on a leaf (Clichy), a grasshopper on a cherry branch (St Louis), a parrot on an orange branch (St Louis) and a bird on a nest (St Louis). Apart from the butterfly motifs, the insect or bird paperweights are believed to be extremely rare if not unique. Some idea of their rarity and value may be gained from some recent sale realizations. A Baccarat butterfly and primrose weight, previously in the collection of Leofredo Maba and sold at Sotheby's in 1963 for £420 ($1008), went for £2050 ($4920) in August 1968. The famous St Louis grasshopper weight sold in May 1968 for £2000 ($4800), and the parrot weight referred to above sold for £3200 ($7680) in August 1968. Both weights were formerly in the Maba collection and fetched £440 ($1056) and £2500 ($6000) respectively when that collection was dispersed in 1963.

Weights depicting fruits or vegetables usually came from St Louis, although an occasional specimen from Baccarat, showing an apple, cherry, peach, pear, red-currant or strawberry, turns up. The only weights in this category attributed to Clichy show pears; the two recorded types feature a single large pear, or two pears suspended from a branch. St Louis produced attractive paperweights showing a mixture of fruits. The most common combinations (but very expensive none the less) feature apples, pears and cherries; rare groups show a striped pippin or a quince among other fruit. An excessively rare example depicted three green figs and three plums; this paperweight is not only believed to be unique but its whereabouts has been unknown for many years. Generally speaking, the fruit paperweights are not so highly regarded as the flower types, probably on aesthetic grounds, but in these times when the market is rising so rapidly on all fronts the increase in price has inevitably affected the fruit and vegetable weights dramatically as well.

One of the rarest types of glass paperweight is the marbrie weight, produced only by St Louis. These weights have a marbled appearance, with ribbon-like festoons set in an opaque white overlay with a small cluster of millefiori canes in the centre. The festoons may be found in red and green, or turquoise or red. A fine example made £1800 ($4320) in the sale of the Gonzales de Cosio collection in July 1967, and a similar one, though not in such good condition, made the same amount at Sotheby's in March 1969. Another type peculiar to St Louis is the celebrated salamander weight, of which two forms are known, either on a solid rock ground or with a hollow interior. A large liver-red salamander weight, sold at Sotheby's in 1963 for £3900 ($9360), fetched £6000 ($14,400) in the same salerooms in May 1968, establishing a new world record price for glass paperweights.

From the prices quoted at random in this chapter it will be gathered that glass paperweights have increased enormously in value in recent years and have now reached the stage where only millionaires can afford to collect them. It is interesting to note that antiquarian interest in the French weights of the mid-nineteenth century did not really begin until after the First World War. In an article in *The Connoisseur* (December 1920) W.H.L. Way commented on the increased interest in paperweights during the previous eight years. Prior to 1912, he stated, 'dated paperweights could be picked up for ten or twelve shillings, whereas now they have risen to four, five and six pounds, and un-dated weights which could be purchased for five shillings have risen to two, three and five pounds, according to beauty of design and good workmanship'. E.M. Elville, in his excellent mono-graph *Paperweights and other Glass Curiosities*, states that the value of paperweights roughly doubled between the world wars, a good dated Baccarat millefiori weight having risen in price by 1939 to £6–£12 ($14–$28), while a fine overlay weight was then valued at £10–£15 ($24–$36). The great collectors in the immediate postwar years, however, boosted the value of the better quality weights enormously. Foremost among these collectors was the late King Farouk, whose agents in London, Spink and Son, were given a virtually unlimited commission from him to buy the best of everything in this line. Since the dispersal of the Farouk and Applewhaite-Abbott collections in the 1950s the present de-cade has seen many fine collections come under the auctioneer's hammer, and items which thirty years ago fetched tens of pounds now rate a hundred times as much.

Undoubtedly the finest glass paperweights were those produced by the French factories, and the value attached to them has inevitably been enhanced by the comparative wealth of literature on the subject. The principal handbook for many years was *Les Presse-Papiers Français* by R. Imbert and Y. Amic, published in 1948, but recently Miss Patricia K. MacCawley of Spink's has produced an exhaustive study under the title of *Antique Glass Paperweights from France* which systematically lists all the known types according to subject, pattern and style. Apart from the text, which is exceptionally clear, the illustrations in colour or black and white are a boon to the collector and will make this book the definitive work on the subject for years to come. Although a fair proportion of French glass paperweights bear the name or initials of the factory, identification is a skill which only comes with years of experience. Moreover, there are later reproductions of inferior workmanship, and it pays to buy from specialist dealers or through the more reputable sale rooms. There are reasonably good millefiori weights which were produced in Millville, New Jersey, and are still being turned out in Murano and China, but whether they will ever attain the dizzy heights of the Baccarat, Clichy and St Louis paperweights is a matter for conjecture.

It is interesting to note that some excellent paperweights have also been produced in the United Kingdom, and are being manufactured to this day. The year 1845, which witnessed the debut of the modern paperweight at the Vienna exhibition, was also the year in which the restrictive Glass Excise was removed in Britain, and at once the glassmakers of that country were encouraged to try their hand at paperweights and similar novelties. It is traditionally believed that the art of manufacturing glass paperweights was introduced to Stourbridge by craftsmen from Clichy. Indeed, there are many similarities between the millefiori weights of Clichy and Stourbridge, though the latter tend to be somewhat larger, with fewer concentric circles and less brilliant colouring. The Stourbridge glassworkers copied their French counterparts in the production of other items with a millefiori decoration, such as ink wells, pen holders and other requisites for the writing desk, but they also went much further in this direction than the French and produced a wide range of articles, from bottles, decanters and wine goblets to doorknobs, candlesticks and oil lamps. English paperweights were usually larger than the average French type, from three and a half to five and a quarter inches in diameter being recorded. A tell-tale feature of the English weights is their slightly raised rim (the French weight having a completely flat base). The English factories also tried their hand at flower and insect weights, but, generally speaking, these are inferior in design and quality to the French types.

A type of paperweight peculiar to the British glass-houses was that made in green bottle glass, with a comparatively high dome and enclosing a representation of a flower or plant growing from a pot, the leaves and petals covered with masses of tiny silvery bubbles. The design was achieved by sprinkling chalk dust on the marver (the base on which the paperweight was built up) and pressing over it a mass of soft green glass. A second layer of molten bottle glass was then pressed over it to enclose the chalk and the action of the heat produced the gaseous bubbles imparting to these weights their silvery, fairy-like appearance when held up to the light. These paperweights were produced in glass factories all over Britain, and may be regarded as a by-product of the period when bottles were still largely made by hand. When bottles began to be machine produced the making of green paperweights died out. At one time these weights were fairly plentiful, but they are seldom seen nowadays, and are attracting the serious attention of collectors, so it is worth hunting through drawers and the proverbial attic to which they may have long been relegated. Very large examples, weighing up to six pounds, were intended for use as door-stops rather than paperweights.

The best examples of modern British weights may definitely be regarded as having antiquarian interest and value already. Two companies in particular are renowned for their paperweights, the Whitefriars Glass Company (formerly Powells of Wealdstone) and the Strathearn Glass Company of Perthshire founded by the Spanish family of Ysart in 1915 and continuing the production of fine glass paperweights in the traditional manner.

Apart from the subject of the paperweight, its size may also have some bearing on its value to the collector. The majority of paperweights are about three inches in diameter, but both smaller and larger weights exist. The small weights, known as miniatures, range in diameter from one and a half to two inches. Elville estimates that about 5 per cent of all millefiori weights were in this category, though miniature flower weights seem to have been a speciality of Baccarat. Not so long ago miniatures were not very highly regarded, but recent prices at auction indicate that, if anything, these small weights, especially the floral ones, rate a premium over the normal-sized examples. The large weights, known as magnums, are about four inches in diameter and were produced by Baccarat and Clichy. Nearly all of them have millefiori patterns, and they, too, are more highly prized than the average-sized paperweights. Magnums in designs other than purely millefiori patterns are extremely rare and fetch thousands of pounds.

5 Porcelain

Of all man-made substances none has ever rivalled gold and silver in intrinsic value to the same extent as porcelain. The fine hard-paste porcelain invented in China more than a thousand years ago evolved over the centuries into a fantastically light yet durable substance: egg-shell in quality yet with the strength to turn a knife-blade. Its delicate underglaze decoration had an almost magical appearance, and it is small wonder that articles in this fascinating material should have taken Europe by storm when they were first imported in the late sixteenth century. It has been recorded that certain pieces in the Imperial Palace bore the Chinese inscription signifying 'To be fondled by His Imperial Majesty', and this indicates the high regard in which fine porcelain was held in China.

Porcelain imported into Europe by the various East India companies was at first reserved for the privileged few who could afford it. The courtly houses of Europe vied with one another in the magnificence of their porcelain dinner services, many of which were specially commissioned from the potteries of Cathay. During the seventeenth century a highly prosperous industry developed for the export of porcelain designed specifically for the European market. The rich merchant classes of the period aped their royal masters in their desire for porcelain. There are numerous stories told concerning the decoration of these export wares, which was done to the customer's choice. Sometimes the Chinese artist copied the instructions he was given too closely—and this accounts for such curiosities as the dinner service bearing a coat of arms and the unintentional inscription—'The Arms of myself and my Wife'.

While the rich bourgeoisie of the seventeenth century were content to import porcelain from China to meet their requirements, the rulers of the European states spent vast sums of money in attempts to discover the secret formula for the manufacture of porcelain. Foremost in the race to probe this secret was the

Elector of Saxony, Augustus the Strong (a reference to his prowess in the bedroom rather than on the battlefield). In his impregnable fortress, the Albrechtsburg, towering above the town of Meissen, he kept the alchemist Johann Friedrich Böttger in semi-imprisonment while he conducted experiments for his royal master. The first goal of these experiments was to discover the philosopher's stone, which would transmute base metal into gold; Böttger, of course, failed in this respect, but he did succeed in discovering the formula for hard-paste porcelain.

Chinese porcelain was compounded of china clay (*kaolin*) and china stone (*petuntse*)—the 'flesh and bones' which give the substance its durability and lightness. Böttger (1682–1719) discovered deposits of felspathic stone which enabled him to emulate the hard-paste of Chinese porcelain. His experiments led to the production of unglazed porcelain by 1708 and a satisfactory glaze. The following year he was able to report that he could produce white porcelain the equal of anything manufactured in China. The Royal Saxon Porcelain Manufactory was established in 1710.

The Saxon factory was soon followed by similar royal establishments in Naples (Capo di Monte) and France (Sèvres). Over a period of more than two centuries all three factories endured many vicissitudes, but all are still in production, though none of them is a royal concern any more; the Meissen factory is now known as the Volks Eigener Betrieb Staatliche Porzellan-Manufaktur since Meissen is in the German Democratic Republic. Despite social and political changes, however, the standard of workmanship and excellence of design have altered little since the days of *Modellmeister* J.J. Kändler, whose famous harlequins and columbines derived from the Commedia dell'Arte now fetch up to five figures when they turn up in the sale room. In the state-owned enterprise of Meissen working methods have hardly changed since the days of the Elector Augustus. Figures and set pieces designed over 200 years ago are still in production. Almost everything is modelled by hand, and more than half the 1000 employees are hand painters—this in spite of the fact that transfer painting has been used in the ceramics industry for 150 years or more. Consequently Meissen figures and dinner sets are extremely expensive. Besides this export controls in East Germany have tended to militate against the ready acceptance of modern Meissen outside Eastern Europe. In 1968, however, the import allowance from East Germany to Britain was substantially raised and a special quota for the Meissen factory was granted, an estimated £30,000 ($72,000) of Meissen porcelain being imported into Britain in 1969.

79

Useful wares such as coffee sets and dinner services are among the more popular Meissen products, but from the investor's viewpoint the various figures and groups are most important. Of these the shepherdesses are perennial favourites, based on models dating back to the early eighteenth century. Another favourite is the rather whimsical monkey bandsman. Meissen have been producing a veritable orchestra of these entrancing figures for more than a century now, and some of the earlier pieces have been known to fetch up to £1000 ($2400) in auction. Current models retail in the United Kingdom at around £60 ($144) each.

The Sèvres factory began operations in 1745 after seven years of experiment and specialized in soft paste (*pâte tendre*) porcelain. By 1790 the Royal factory was virtually bankrupt, and the Revolution did not help matters. Under the patronage of Napoleon its fortunes improved somewhat. Alexandre Brongniart controlled it from 1800 to 1847, and under his influence Sèvres products continued to improve technically. Within four years of his retirement, however, standards had begun to decline noticeably and did not begin to improve until the latter years of the century. Since 1876 the Sèvres factory has been located at St Cloud, and today produces some fine wares in the medium-price range.

Without doubt, however, Britain at present is playing a leading role in the porcelain world, and pride of place must be given to the products of the Royal Worcester Porcelain Factory, which, as regards the models in limited editions, are in a class by themselves. It seems curious that the British monarchy was never preoccupied, like its European counterparts, with the manufacture of fine porcelain. While the King of Naples and the Elector of Saxony were losing fortunes in their quest for the elusive substance, Britain's Georges were content to leave this to private enterprise. This explains to some extent the ultimate failure of the Chelsea, Bow and mysterious 'Girl in a Swing' factories which flourished brilliantly if briefly in the mid-eighteenth century.

Another of the pioneer factories, Lund's of Bristol, was taken over in 1751 by a syndicate of Worcester businessmen led by the physician and amateur potter, Dr John Wall. The equipment and craftsmen of the Bristol pottery were removed to Worcester, where production had commenced by 1752. This was the beginning of an enterprise in Worcester which has lasted to this day and, indeed, has gone from strength to strength.

The company underwent several changes of ownership over the two centuries of its existence, and its fortunes varied accordingly. The Golden Age of Worcester porcelain was the First or 'Doctor Wall' period, which lasted till 1783, seven years after the doctor's death. The wares of this period are characterized by the neat, meticulous potting of the fine, rather hard paste, whose composition and consistency remained constant over the years, in a good range of attractive shapes and with a wide variety of decorative styles. The decoration was subtle and elegant, never garish or ostentatious, and the colours were soft and diffused. In view of Worcester's later history it is interesting to note that very few figures were produced, the emphasis being on dinner services, plates, dishes and a whole host of smaller items such as salad bowls, egg cups, patty pans and mustard pots.

In 1783 the factory was purchased by its London agent, Thomas Flight, for his sons John and Joseph. Under new management it went through a period marked by innovation and experiment, in a bid to fight the fierce competition of the Staffordshire potteries. John Flight died in 1791, and his surviving brother went into partnership with Martin Barr, hence the mark 'Flight and Barr' on wares of the period 1792–1807. Thereafter the marks changed frequently as the partnership was rearranged: Barr, Flight and Barr (1807–13), or Flight, Barr and Barr (1813–40).

The gradual deterioration in standards during the Second Period was paralleled everywhere else in the English ceramic industry, though Worcester porcelain was probably not as badly affected as many others. It was marked, however, by poorer quality in the paste, resulting in a chalky appearance, the mechanical nature of the painting and the substitution of a flatter, more brassy mercury gilding for the old gilding—a compound of ground gold leaf and honey—for which 'Dr Wall' porcelain was famous. Nevertheless, many fine pieces were produced in the Flight Period, characterized by the excellence of the birds and scenery, hand-painted by factory craftsmen who were recognized as artists in their own right. Indeed, the chief interest of Worcester porcelain of this period lies in the excellence of the painting rather than the paste: among the artists employed were the celebrated Thomas Baxter, Moses Webster, Robert Brewer and William Billingsley.

In 1840 the company merged with a rival concern founded by Robert Chamberlain, Dr Wall's first apprentice. He set up his own company in 1783, and over a period of almost sixty years it, too, underwent several changes of partnership and name. After a turbulent period of eleven years during which the company probably reached its nadir, a new partnership was evolved between W.H. Kerr (related by marriage to the Chamberlains) and R.W. Binns. A revival in the fortunes of the company coincided with their moderate success at the Great Exhibition of 1851 and the Dublin

Exhibition which followed two years later. Under Messrs Kerr and Binns something of the pristine glory of Worcester was recaptured. An outstanding product of this period was the so-called 'Shakespeare Service'—a dessert service for twenty-four, the comports supported by figures from *A Midsummer Night's Dream*. The decoration on this ceramic *tour de force* was the work of W.B. Kirk, son of Kirk the famous Dublin sculptor, and a celebrated artist in his own right.

Artists of the calibre of Plant, Williams and Doe were greatly helped and inspired by the work of their predecessors and the classic products of the eighteenth-century factories. This is not to say that they slavishly imitated the ornamental wares of Meissen, Sèvres and Limoges; rather they maintained the traditions of eighteenth-century craftsmanship and added to it their own star quality.

In 1862 the factory was reconstituted as a joint-stock company under the style of the Worcester Royal Porcelain Company Limited, the name by which it is known to this day. As far as the output of the factory was concerned the change of name was purely incidental, and one can trace the continuous development of Worcester porcelain from the mid-nineteenth century onwards without the slightest interruption. As the century wore on the products of the Worcester factory became increasingly elaborate in decoration and extravagant in gilding. Although the ornamental wares of this period are altogether too lavish for modern taste, it should be noted that Worcester porcelain was invariably judged the finest among its peers. At the Vienna International Exhibition of 1873, for example, British porcelain surpassed its Continental rivals, and the products of Worcester and Minton, in fact, tied for the highest award. At the Paris Exhibition five years later Worcester was not only awarded the Gold Medal but R.W. Binns was given the Légion d'Honneur. Compared with the products of the 'antique' period, the table wares and figures of the late nineteenth century are undervalued at present. Here, therefore, is plenty of scope for the astute collector.

In great demand, and rightly so, are the remarkable reticulated pieces produced in the last decade of the century by George Owen, lacy, delicate and fragile, with every tiny shaped aperture separately pierced. The best examples of Owen's work were double-walled, the inner wall solid and the outer one perforated, and usually enamelled in brilliant colours. Owen's pieces were invariably signed by him, but caution should be exercised, since cheaper imitations were subsequently manufactured by semi-mechanical processes.

82

Incidentally, a problem raised in the manufacture of Owen's 'pierced porcelain' was that the clay had to be kept at a consistent humidity while being worked. Owen overcame this problem by devising a special box whose humid atmosphere kept the clay moist and plastic. This device has been used more recently in the production of the intricate bird groups modelled by Dorothy Doughty. The transfer of the delicate leaves and blossoms, forming the background to the birds, is carried out with the same skill, patience and precision which characterized Owen's work.

At the end of the nineteenth century there was relatively little public demand for ornamental porcelain, such as figures and centrepieces, and Worcester accordingly produced few of these. On the other hand, the demand for richly decorated services was unabated, and the company spared no pains to secure the talent of such fashionable artists as Sir Lawrence Alma-Tadema, who designed a magnificent dinner service for the Queen of the Netherlands.

But, as always, Worcester relied mainly on the artistic brilliance of its own employees. In the 1890s the *maestro* of the painting studios was W.A. Hawkins, best remembered for his astonishingly faithful miniature reproductions of such masterpieces as Gainsborough's *Blue Boy* and Goya's *Duke of Wellington*. The fine tradition of Baxter, Brewer and Hawkins is continued today by artists like Harry Davis, at the time of writing the oldest and longest-serving member in the Company. Mr Davis entered Worcester's employment in the 1890s, and for many years has been responsible for the delicately hand-painted decoration on numerous special orders. In 1926, for example, he decorated a dinner service of 300 pieces for the Maharajah of Nawanagar (better known in cricket circles as 'Ranji'), with views of the Maharajah's palaces in India and with outstanding English scenes, including Ranji's gardens at Staines. This service cost £7000 more than forty years ago (about £30,000 ($72,000) in today's debased currency), but undoubtedly it would fetch far more were it ever to come on the market.

In the immediate postwar years Harry Davis painted a dinner service of 300 pieces for the Maharajah of Baroda and, in 1956, a magnificent service of 1344 pieces (weighing four tons!) for the Coronation of King Mahendra of Nepal. Among the individual items of note which he decorated were a vase presented to Sir Winston Churchill featuring an eighteenth-century view of Worcester Cathedral, and, in 1965, an ornamental loving cup presented, on the occasion of their golden wedding, to the Duke and Duchess of Portland by the tenants of the Welbeck Abbey estate.

This elegant vase, depicting the Duke's favourite sports of wood-cock shooting and salmon fishing, demonstrated that the skill and craftsmanship of this veteran artist were enhanced rather than diminished with the years, and is a worthy match for that elegant Roman vase which immortalized the Duke's ancestor who once owned it.

The longevity of Worcester's employees is also demonstrated in the case of the Stinton family. John Stinton, a notable painter of Highland cattle and ruined castles around the turn of the century, celebrated his hundredth birthday in 1954, though he retired from active work some twenty years earlier. His brother, James, specialized in painting game birds, while his son, Harry, only re-tired in 1951 at the age of 81. Their ancestor, Henry Stinton, was an employee of Flight, Barr & Barr in 1815, and a good example of his work is still extant in the Dyson Perrins Museum at Wor-cester.

Continuity with the craftsmanship of the past is evinced at executive level as well. The Managing Director of the Worcester Company from 1914 till 1927, for example, was Gilbert Solon, the son of the famous Marc-Louis Solon who grew up in the traditions of Empire Sèvres and migrated to England after the Franco-Prussian War, to serve Mintons as a *pâte-sur-pâte* artist of the high-est repute. Gilbert Solon's brother, L.V. Solon, became Art Director at Mintons in 1909.

It must not be imagined that Worcester was concerned solely with painting on porcelain, although the universal tendency, in the early years of this century, seems to have been to regard porce-lain merely as a medium for fine painting. The emphasis shifted from the decoration to the porcelain itself with the revival of in-terest in ornamental figures in the 1930s.

As has been mentioned in the opening chapter of this book, in the early years of this century an undemanding and undiscrimin-ating public had a bad effect generally on manufacturers in the fields of ceramics, as in textiles and metalware. At Worcester tra-ditions of fine craftsmanship were fortunately maintained in the production of special services, but as regards the 'bread and butter' work the company could do little more than repeat old-tried favourites and earlier lines which enjoyed perennial popu-larity. The renaissance in porcelain as an art form was due largely to the fine-art publisher Alex Dickins, who encouraged ceramic artists such as Aline Ellis and Gwendolyn Parnell to produce figures in their studio potteries. The experimental figures by these artist-potters were limited in production, and today they are eagerly sought by the *aficionados* of fine modern porcelain.

84

Their products, however, pale by comparison with the works of the late Dorothy Doughty. In 1934, largely as a result of prompting by Dickins, Worcester produced a dessert service decorated with motifs taken from the monumental *Birds of America* by John James Audubon. Simultaneously Worcester commissioned Miss Doughty to execute models of American birds which were originally intended as ornaments for the mantelpiece. She began work on the First Series in 1933, but the first models, the Redstarts on Hemlock, were not ready for production till 1935. The Redstarts were the only models designed from photographs; all of the subsequent Dorothy Doughty birds were modelled from life, and she travelled many thousands of miles in quest of the originals. This resulted in greater realism not only in the modelling but in the positioning of the birds in their most characteristic attitudes. It is interesting to study the early Doughty birds and note their rapid development, as both the designer and the Worcester craftsmen experimented with new techniques in modelling and casting, evolving by trial and error the masterpieces which remain unrivalled in the world of porcelain. The modelling of the background foliage and flowers called for a very high degree of skill. Their appearance is often quite deceptive, and few people looking at the Chiff-chaff on Hogweed would realize that the apparently simple arrangement of small clusters of flowers on stalks represents the acme of technical achievement.

It would be difficult to say whether the birds or the flowers inspired Miss Doughty more. She set herself extremely high standards in constantly striving to imbue her creations with realism, and it is to their credit that the artist-craftsmen of Worcester interpreted her models so successfully. In the case of some of the earlier models, anything up to three years might elapse between Miss Doughty's preliminary sketches and the issue of the birds from the factory. The American birds were important dollar-earners, and their production was carried on during the Second World War as far as possible. Worcester, however, was engaged on important war work, producing insulators for the Air Ministry and laboratory equipment, while Miss Doughty, appropriately enough, was employed in the experimental side of aircraft production. Consequently no new models appeared after 1945, and it was not, in fact, till 1950 that the Second Series of American birds could be released.

Though it is to the genius and artistry of Miss Doughty that the birds owe their existence, credit ought also to be given to the large team of experts, artists and technicians assembled by Worcester in order to bring the series to fruition. Harry Davis was largely responsible for surmounting the practical problems raised by the colouring of flower and plumage and, till 1955, had overall control in maintaining the colour standards. Ronald van Ruyckevelt, of the Royal College of Art, was appointed general organizer to superintend the preliminary work involved on each model, and under his supervision the time elapsing between preliminary modelling and actual production was shortened considerably. Mr van Ruyckevelt has subsequently become an accomplished modeller in his own right. It would be impossible to cast each model in a single mould, because of the intricacies and complexities of these pieces. It is necessary to dissect the model into a number of components which can be moulded separately. The responsibility for dissecting the American bird models was given to F.M. Gertner, Worcester's chief modeller, whose own Historic Figures are also in considerable demand.

The average bird model required about twenty moulds, though the Magnolia Warblers of 1950 needed as many as fifty-seven. Although modern equipment and better working conditions have improved the industry enormously, many of the processes involved in the production of ornamental porcelain rely on the skills of individual craftsmen, and these men and women are still as important as they were two centuries ago. Worcester and, to a much lesser extent, Mintons are virtually alone today in maintaining the high traditions of yesteryear. Royal Worcester has, in fact, never produced anything other than porcelain, a substance prized by kings and princes and now avidly collected by persons with the taste to appreciate it and the money to afford it.

This has not always been the case, however, and it should be noted that changing fashions in interior decoration towards the end of the eighteenth century led to a marked decline in the popularity of porcelain. It did not revive till the 1870s, and then interest in old porcelain tended to be rather academic, the pursuit of *savants* rather than the general public. It is only since the Dorothy Doughty birds in the 1930s that ornamental porcelain has enjoyed a revival in fortune, and this is now reaching such proportions that its previous, eighteenth-century popularity is being overshadowed.

This revival in popularity undoubtedly had its beginnings in America, a country which had no traditions of porcelain manufacture to speak of. It must not be imagined, however, that the Doughty birds were not popular in the country of their manufacture. The advent of the Second World War, so soon after the inception of the first series, followed by 'export only' restrictions in the immediate postwar years, had a marked effect on interest in modern porcelain in Britain. During the past fifteen years, however, interest in the ornamental wares produced by Worcester in particular has increased enormously.

Shortly before her untimely death in 1962 Miss Doughty completed a series of models of British birds. These are produced at the rate of two or three a year, and it will be well into the 1970s before they have all been released. The intrinsic value of the materials used, the skill and craftsmanship born of long years of experience, and the incomparable brilliance of Miss Doughty's artistry are combined in the production of articles which obviously are not cheap. Current models retail at prices between £400 ($960) and £850 ($2040). Since they have no scrap value (as has gold or silver), how can one be sure that their value will be maintained, let alone increase? The caprices of fashion are such that one can never be certain on that score, but since each model is produced in a strictly limited edition (after which the moulds are destroyed) the collector may have confidence in the material he is collecting. This may even be an advantage over antique porcelain, where the quantity of similar material in private hands or coming on the market is imponderable. As the demand for fine modern porcelain grows (and I am confident that it has not attained the acme of popularity by a long way) the value of those limited editions will inevitably rise.

Probably the most outstanding example of the way in which Doughty birds produced in the past thirty years have increased in value concerns the American Bob Quail which appeared in 1940. Although extremely attractive, this pair was the least successful of the first series. As Miss Doughty herself wrote: 'Alex Dickins had asked me to make a sportsman's model to go in a man's study. "Let us have a Bob White Quail as a favourite game bird, but without any flowers. Flowers are for ladies' models. This one is for their husbands." I did not like this "no flower" idea, and for life and beauty I gave the little hen Quail a pair of tiny mottled babies. The result was that no sportsman wanted the model, because when there are chicks it is the close season for shooting. And so this edition, too, died young just because I had made a mistake!'

As a result, only twenty-two pairs were sold before the edition was discontinued. In 1965 a sum reputedly in the region of $50,000 (£20,000) was paid for a pair of Bob White Quail, rivalling the records achieved by the best eighteenth-century Meissen figures. Overpage is a table of the American Birds of Dorothy Doughty which has been compiled by Mrs Moira Gibson of the Royal Worcester Porcelain Company. It shows, where possible, the original

Name of Model	Original S. price (shillings)	Highest price at auction $	(1968) Latest price best $	(1968) Latest price damaged $
American Redstarts and Hemlock—pair		17,500	17,500	
American Goldfinches and Thistle—pair		4,750	4,750	
Blue Birds and Apple Blossom—pair		7,500	7,500	2,250
Virginian Cardinals and Orange Blossom—pair		6,600	6,600	2,750
Single Indigo Bunting Cock on Plum Twigs		16,000	16,000	
Baltimore Orioles and Tulip Tree—Cock	360s	5,700	5,700	4,800
,, ,, ,, —Hen	360s	5,700	5,700	4,800
Chickadees and Larch—pair		3,000		2,000
Crab Apple Sprays and Butterfly (1)	565s	2,600	2,600	
,, ,, ,, (2)	565s	2,600	2,600	
Mocking Birds and Peach Blossom—Cock	595s	5,400	5,400	3,600
,, ,, ,, —Hen	595s	5,400	5,400	3,600
Bob White Quail		36,000	30,000	
Apple Blossom Sprays (2 bees)	515s	1,000		1,000
,, ,, (1 bee)	515s	1,000		1,000
Indigo Buntings and Blackberry—pair		2,500	2,500	1,900
Orange Blossom Sprays (1)	600s	3,800	1,900	
,, ,, (2)	600s	3,800	1,900	
Humming Birds and Fuchsia—Cock	700s	2,700	1,400	
,, ,, ,, —Hen	700s	2,700	1,400	
Mexican Feijoa and Ladybirds (1)	700s	4,700	3,000	
,, ,, ,, (2)	700s	4,700	3,000	
Magnolia Warblers and Magnolia—Cock	1480s	8,700	8,700	
,, ,, ,, —Hen	1480s	8,700	8,700	
Golden Crowned Kinglets and Noble Pine—single	420s	3,000	3,000	
,, ,, ,, —double	420s	3,000	3,000	
Vireos and Swamp Azalea—Cock	450s	1,600	1,600	1,200
,, ,, ,, —Hen	450s	1,600	1,600	1,200
Yellow-headed Blackbirds and Spiderwort—Cock	755s	1,755	1,755	
,, ,, ,, ,, —Hen	755s	1,755	1,755	
Blue-grey Gnatcatchers and Dogwood—Single	595s	3,800	3,800	
,, ,, ,, —Double	595s	3,800	3,800	
Myrtle Warblers and Weeping Cherry—Cock	550s	2,100	2,100	900
,, ,, ,, —Hen	550s	2,100	2,100	900
Bewick's Wrens and Yellow Jasmine—Cock	550s	2,600	2,600	1,300
,, ,, ,, —Hen	550s	2,600	2,600	1,300
Scarlet Tanagers and White Oak—Cock	700s	1,800	1,800	1,500
,, ,, ,, —Hen	700s	1,800	1,800	1,500
Oven Birds with Crested Iris and Ladys Slipper —Cock	600s	3,000	3,000	2,200
—Hen	600s	3,000	3,000	2,200
Parula Warblers and Sweet Bay—Cock	500s	2,600	2,000	
,, ,, ,, —Hen	500s	2,600	2,000	
Yellow-throats and Water Hyacinth—Cock	650s	2,900	2,900	
,, ,, ,, ,, —Hen	650s			
Phoebes and Flame Vine—Mother	650s	4,200	4,200	
,, ,, —Chick	650s	4,200	4,200	

Name of Model	Original S. price (shillings)	Highest price at auction $	(1968) Latest price best $	(1968) Latest price damaged $
Elf Owl and Saguaro—single	1600s	1,200	1,200	
Cactus Wrens and Prickly Pear—Cock	1000s	1,400	1,400	1,200
„ „ „ —Hen	1000s	1,400	1,400	1,200
Canyon Wrens and Wild Lupin—Cock	700s	1,000	1,000	
„ „ „ —Hen	700s	1,000	1,000	
Hooded Warblers and Cherokee Rose—Cock	900s	2,300	2,300	2,100
„ „ „ „ —Hen	900s	2,300	2,300	2,100
Vermilion Flycatchers and Pussy Willow—Cock	820s	1,100	1,100	
„ „ „ „ —Hen	820s	1,100	1,100	
Audubon's Warblers and Palo Verdi—Cock	900s	1,450	1,450	
„ „ „ „ —Hen	900s	1,450	1,450	
Mountain Bluebirds and Spleenwort Niger—Cock	600s	1,100	1,100	
„ „ „ „ —Hen	600s	1,100	1,100	
Cerulean Warblers and Red Maple—Cock	902s	1,250	1,250	
„ „ „ „ —Hen	902s	1,250	1,250	
Lazuli Buntings and Choke Cherry—Cock	900s	2,000	1,800	1,700
„ „ „ „ —Hen	900s	2,000	1,800	1,700

retail prices of the figures with the record prices and highest 1968 prices attained in each case. These statistics are self-explanatory; it will be seen that anyone who purchased the American Birds series as they were issued would have built up a very nice investment over the past thirty-odd years. Even allowing for the fall in the value of money over this period, I doubt whether any other class of object would have shown the same return for a proportionate capital outlay.

DORIS LINDNER ANIMALS

In a less expensive category than the Dorothy Doughty birds, though no less appealing and aesthetically satisfying, are the animal figures modelled for Royal Worcester by Miss Doris Lindner. Miss Lindner was born in South Wales and first studied animal painting at Calderon's School of Animal Painting in London. Here she received thorough instruction in anatomy and the study of animals from life. Later she attended art courses at St Martins in London, as well as the British Academy in Rome. For forty years she has been a practising sculptress, concentrating almost entirely on animals. Her earliest work for Royal Worcester consisted of a series of dog portraits and studies of a Fox and a Hound, produced in 1931. A series of small equestrian statuettes, including

'Cantering to the Post' and 'Polo Player', gave her an opportunity to express her love of horses and to bring more action into her modelling.

Miss Lindner now produces two models a year for Royal Worcester, and in the course of these projects she has travelled extensively in order to study the animals in their natural surroundings. For her recent models of a Charollais Bull and a Brahman Bull she spent some time in France and Texas respectively. Miss Lindner spends many hours sketching and photographing the animals from different angles before she begins work on the actual models. This care and attention to detail is evident too in her equestrian figures such as the racehorses Arkle and Hyperion. One of her most recent equestrian statuettes is a spirited model of the Duke of Edinburgh mounted on a polo pony. The preliminary work for this model took her to Windsor, where she made sketches of the Duke at polo matches. In the Royal Mews at Windsor Castle she studied the ponies at close quarters and handled the harness and polo equipment. A sitting with the Duke himself was also required before the model could be completed. The result, interpreted by Worcester's craftsmen, is a masterpiece and a worthy match for the equestrian statuette of the Queen (then Princess Elizabeth) which Doris Lindner produced in 1947. This figure, showing the Princess in the uniform of the Grenadier Guards mounted on her police horse Tommy at her first Trooping of the Colour, was released in a limited edition of 100 and retailed twenty years ago at £120 ($288). It is interesting to note that, at Sotheby's in 1968, model number 92 fetched £1800 (($4320).

Doris Lindner animals are usually produced in limited editions of 500, but, of late, these editions have been selling out in record time, and when they do come back on the market have been resold at a substantial premium.

OTHER WORCESTER FIGURES

Closely associated with Dorothy Doughty during the last ten years of her life was Ronald Van Ruyckevelt. As has been mentioned earlier, he was involved in superintending the production of the third series of American birds and the current models of British birds. He is an accomplished artist in his own right, however, and his first efforts for Worcester were a series of small American birds which have been extremely successful.

Subsequently he produced limited editions of tropical fishes and flowers. Currently he is working on a series of American game birds, and his pheasants and mallard duck are already in production. In designing these birds Mr Van Ruyckevelt paid several visits to the United States to study them in their natural habitat.

His wife, Ruth, has been engaged in the creation of a series of figures of ladies. These attractive models, depicting various facets of nineteenth-century American costume, range in retail price from £60 ($144) for a figure of a girl in late Victorian tennis costume to £189 ($456) for the group of figures known as 'The Tea Party'. In the latter group every intricate detail was correct, down to the miniature cups and saucers on the table.

ROYAL DOULTON

Although Royal Doulton's reputation has largely been built on their production of earthenware, sanitary fittings, electric insulators and laboratory equipment, they have also been deeply involved in the production of fine china since 1884, when Henry Doulton established a china works at Burslem. In recent years they have produced a large number of figurines which sell in the region of £10–£15 ($24–$36) when current, and have attracted a large following. Doulton's entered the field of limited editions in the 1950s, when they produced Princess Badoura, an exotic figure seated upon a richly caparisoned elephant. Finely modelled animals—lion, tiger, leopard and elephant—were also produced in Doulton's Prestige Figure series. Among the human figures in this range are the Moor, Jack Point, King Charles and the Old King. More elaborate was the dazzling equestrian figure of St George and then the spirited Matador and Bull which appeared in 1963. The most recent figure group in this series is Doulton's Indian Brave sculpted by Mrs Peggy Davies. The model is of a Sioux warrior in the colourful dress of the Sun Dance ceremony mounted on a pony. No fewer than fifty-nine moulds were required for this figure, and the feathers were individually made from a special clay to ensure fineness and accuracy in reproduction. A figure of this complexity necessitated the installation of a special electric-fired kiln to meet the exacting requirements and preserve precise control in all six firing stages.

Royal Doulton's prestige models, Matador and Bull and North American Indian, retailed at £590 ($1416) and £446 ($1070) respectively in editions of 500 each.

OTHER FACTORIES

Mintons of Stoke-on-Trent concentrate nowadays on the production of fine china tableware, but it should be noted that the vase

91

produced in 1954 for presentation to the Queen by the British Pottery Manufacturers' Federation was largely modelled and decorated under the supervision of the late John W. Wadsworth of Mintons. Incorporated with this vase were exquisite models of the Queen's Beasts, ten in number, each resplendent in authentic colourings with the appropriate armorial shield. After production of the vase was completed Mintons executed a limited edition of the Queen's Beasts from the original models by James Woodford. The *Pottery Gazette and Glass Trade Review* (October 1955) commented on these figures,

'Symbolizing as they do the ancient and chivalrous ancestry of the British Crown, and coupled with a manufacturer's name that is itself a hallmark of quality, there is little doubt that these ornaments will have an immediate value in excess of their list price, which has yet to be fixed. Assuming that production will cease after a specified period, their antique value, which in the ordinary course of events will begin to take effect around the early years of the twenty-first century, should be considerable. To what extent this possibility will influence buyers today must remain a matter for speculation.'

There were, in fact, some 150 sets of the Beasts, and each figure retailed initially at £18 15s ($45). But they were quickly snapped up, and the complete set today has a market value well in excess of the £187 10s ($450) originally charged, proving that it is not necessary to wait till the early years of the twenty-first century for 'antique value' to take effect.

Coalport are making fine reproductions in the old Coalbrookdale style of flower-encrusted china ornaments. The Spode factory at Stoke-on-Trent recently produced a Churchill commemorative vase in a limited edition of 125 pieces, selling at 125 guineas ($315). These were all sold within three days. To meet popular demand Spode's subsequently produced a Churchill plate in an edition of 5000 copies at 19 guineas ($23.88).

On the American scene, the talented sculptor-ceramist Edward Marshall Boehm—naturalist, ornithologist and cattle-breeder of note—began producing fine porcelain figures and animal models about 1953. Many of his early pieces, which originally sold for a few dollars, now fetch thousands from his many admirers in the United States. Modelling from the exotic birds he collects and rears in his own enormous aviaries overlooking the Delaware River in Trenton, New Jersey, his works are masterpieces of ceramic art. Although they are available in Britain, since his subjects are mostly American, they have not yet received full recognition there for their beauty and the artistic skill of their creation or for their investment value.

One pair of birds, 'Eastern Bluebirds and Rhododendrons', was sold by Thomas Goode, London's leading porcelain dealer, in 1964 for £730 ($1752) shortly before the edition of 100 pairs was completed. This pair is now changing hands in America for around $6000. Even the limited edition of 750 of the 'Meadow Lark', a few of which Goode's sold in London for £143 ($343) each, are now being bought by American collectors for as much as $2000 (£800).

There is little chance of the potential demand being easily satisfied, for the skills required to make the finest examples are so rare in this age of mass production, and the number of collectors is increasing so rapidly, that there are simply not enough to satisfy their needs. Things of beauty they are indeed, and it is a rare investment which gives pleasure and enjoyment to the investor while it is appreciating in value.

6 Furniture

Although the more orthodox antique dealers may be prepared to make some leeway, chronologically speaking, in classifying as antique such things as silver, glassware, porcelain and pictures, on one subject they remain fairly adamant—and that is furniture. The Antiques in Britain Fairs, for example, will permit the sale of silver, glassware and porcelain up to 1850 and pictures as late as 1890, but 1830 remains the limit as far as furniture is concerned. The layman must often be puzzled by the rigid adherence to this date. Why is it that 1830 is so significant anyway? The year in which King George IV died is regarded, in the history of taste, as marking the end of the Regency period—even though for the past decade George had ruled as King and not as Prince Regent. The fashions which had been established during his Regency (1810–20) lingered on until the end of the reign. Indeed, Regency fashions did not die out immediately with the accession of William IV, but already great social and political changes were sweeping over Britain. Although they were not crystallized until the middle of the century, it is customary in the world of fashion to speak of the Victorian era as though it had commenced seven years before the young queen ascended the throne in 1837.

While fashions in ceramics, glass and metal wares did not change much before the Great Exhibition of 1851, the styles, techniques and even the materials of furniture had been undergoing radical alteration from the end of the eighteenth century. The rapid growth of economic prosperity which came in the 1830s, when Britain was the first European country to benefit from the Industrial Revolution, stimulated a tremendous demand for furniture. People were earning good wages and began to marry younger: setting up home meant the acquisition of furniture, and no other traditional craft received such a boost. The tremendous demand, however, imposed a terrible strain on the furniture-makers. Overnight a craft was transformed into a major industry.

Although the biggest and most successful of the late eighteenth-century furniture-makers, such as Thomas Chippendale, sometimes employed hundreds of people, the vast majority of the manufacturers at the turn of the century operated quite small establishments, often consisting of a handful of skilled craftsmen—joiner, cabinet-maker and upholsterer with their apprentices. In the chapter on Victoriana I have already mentioned the astonishing growth of the population in the early years of the nineteenth century; but the wealth of the country increased at an even greater rate. The value of British exports in 1800 has been estimated at £34 million; by 1830 this figure had doubled, and by the time of the Great Exhibition it stood at almost £200 million. It was the rise of a new bourgeoisie which had the most profound effect on the production of the sort of furniture likely to concern the collector today. The few humble sticks possessed by the young mill-hand and his wife were not made to last, any more than is the cheap plywood furniture of today; but the new middle classes of the 1830s were intent on aping the manners and the fashions of the nobility, and, moreover, had the money to indulge this taste.

In order to cope with the demand for high-quality furniture the manufacturers not only increased the number of their employees but sought ways of further increasing output by the use of mechanical devices and by the labour-saving techniques of mass production. Unfortunately furniture does not lend itself well to mass production, and inevitably the standards of craftsmanship and the enduring qualities which one looks for in good cabinet-making were sacrificed in the process. Because the traditional timbers, oak, beech, elm, yew, walnut and imported hardwoods like mahogany and rosewood were not really suitable for mechanized furniture-making, softwoods were used increasingly for cheap, painted furniture. This was the era in which the retail furniture supplier emerged, who bought vast quantities of chairs, tables, beds and wardrobes from the wholesaler, who, in turn, got them from the factory. The direct contact between the furniture maker and the consumer was almost eliminated. This pattern of furniture production and distribution has continued down to the present day, and is economically inevitable.

The old method of direct contact between manufacturer and consumer was not, however, entirely extinguished. Where it survived, the best traditions of custom-built pieces were maintained, and examples of furniture made to a specific order after 1830 may be as interesting to the connoisseur as anything produced before that date. The personal link between manufacturer and customer should not be underestimated: much of the lasting appeal of antique furniture stems from the fact that the nobility brought their innate sense of good taste to bear on the pieces they commissioned. It was quite usual for lengthy consultations to take place between a cabinet-maker and his client before a piece of furniture was finally evolved. (This intimate link survived somewhat longer in the country districts, and even today there are small enterprises which can and do produce some excellent furniture to a customer's requirements.) Even the largest of the London manufacturers continued to produce a certain amount of custom-built furniture; and as the century wore on and the general level of prosperity rose the demand for the better-quality furniture increased steadily. Thus, from the second half of the nineteenth century down to the present day, manufacturers such as Heals and Gillows (later Waring and Gillow) have produced top-quality, hand-made furniture for those customers prepared to pay for it. There is a great difference between the elegant pieces produced by the most fashionable of the London firms and the humble items produced by the small provincial craftsman, but they had one thing in common: they were produced by men who took a pride in their work. Both may be desirable to the collector today, because quality, craftsmanship and restrained good taste are the most important criteria to apply to furniture of any period.

It is interesting to note the extent to which English furniture and furniture making dominated the American scene up to the 1870s if not later. During the colonial period (prior to 1783) the rich planters and wealthier colonists imported their furniture direct from England, and this practice continued for at least a hundred years after the American colonies won their independence. An indigenous furniture industry existed from fairly early times, but manufacturers slavishly imitated the patterns laid down by their more fashionable English counterparts. Apart from a few typically American types of furniture, such as the rocking-chair and the Pennsylvania slat-back chair, the styles in furniture closely corresponded to English or French Empire. Even a century ago American labour was more expensive than British, and the American retailers found it cheaper to import furniture from England than have it manufactured in their own country. However, the export of furniture did not operate in the opposite direction at this date, and this accounts for the relative scarcity of good-quality American furniture of the early and mid-Victorian period in Britain or the Continent of Europe. A London Depot of American Furniture was, however, opened in 1882, and from then on it became increasingly popular in Britain.

French furniture had always been fashionable with the upper

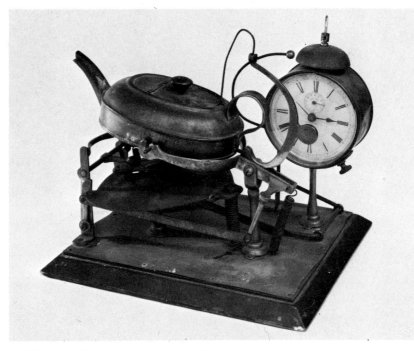

1   Victorian alarm clock cum tea-maker

2   Victorian goffering iron and three charcoal irons

4   Lock-stitch sewing machine by William Jones, *c.* 1879

5   Late Victorian tricycle made by Singer of Coventry, England

6 Victorian blanket-washing stomper

7 Early Victorian reading candelabra in the form of Classical four-branch
   adjustable oil lamps with open-work terminals, each fitted with a chain
   extinguisher, a pair of snuffers, a probe and a pair of tweezers

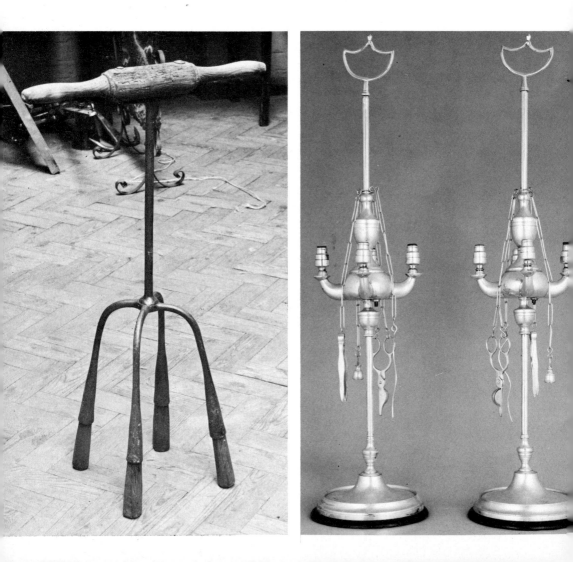

8 Rare Fabergé piece. Pale-green amazonite birds have eyes set with cabochon rubies and chased red gold talons. The food tray contains gold seeds and the domed silver-wire cage is fitted with a removable tray at the base

9 Easter eggs, in a limited edition with various 'surprises' inside, made in silver, silver-gilt and gold by Stuart Devlin, 1968

11   Sterling-silver sugar bowl *c.* 1902 made by W. Hutton and Sons, Ltd

12   Silver coffee set by Jean Puiforcat, 1930

13 Table bell with silver body and silver-gilt rough-cast handle by Stuart Devlin, 1965

14 Striped gilt cigarette box by Gerald Benney, 1964

15 Gilt textured beakers and decanter stoppers by Gerald Benney, 1963

16 Vase by Emile Gallé, 1878

17 Late nineteenth-century glass vases by
Thomas Webb & Sons

18   Tiffany Studio: 'Dragonfly' lamp designed by Clara Driscoll *c.* 1900

19   Tiffany favrile gold 'Jack-in-the-Pulpit' vase *c.* 1900

20   Tiffany paperweight vase *c.* 1900

Opposite

23 *Torque* recent design by Pau[l]
Schulze for Steuben Glass, New
York; although this piece i[s]
unique, Steuben are continuing
with designs of a similar abstrac[t]
nature

21 Large scent bottle, plain glass decorated in black. Probably French, *c.* 1930

22 *Romeo and Juliet* glass design by George Thompson, engraving design by
Tom Vincent, produced for Steuben Glass, New York, in a limited edition
of ten

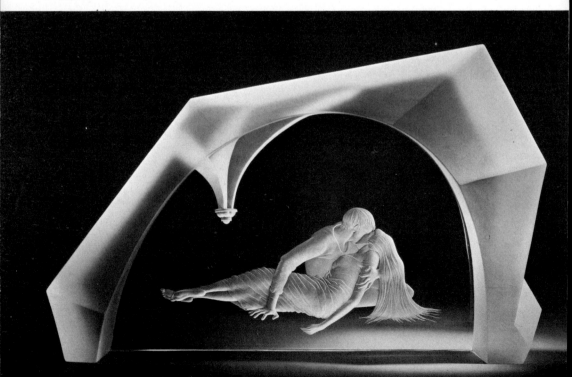

24 a Clichy blue-ground paperweight
   b St Louis fruit weight
   c St Louis fruit weight
   d Baccarat butterfly weight
   e St Louis fruit weight
   f Clichy colour-ground weight

25 a Baccarat close millefiori weight
      b Baccarat periwinkle weight
      c St Louis crown weight
      d Rare cherry weight
      e St Louis turnip weight·
      f Rare Baccarat strawberry weight

26 Salt-glaze vase decorated by Florence E. Barlow, with two oval panels of quail in green and white pâte-sur-pâte, separated by branches on which are perched bluebirds on a buff ground of incised foliage

27 These hand-modelled pieces are revivals of the original Coalbrookdale ware and are being made today in limited editions of 250 each at Coalport. In fine bone china, each has raised floral decoration in white or colour

28 Mallard duck and drake, modelled by Ronald van Ruyckevelt produced by Worcester Royal Porcelain Co., 1968, in a limited edition of 500

29 *Brahman Bull* modelled by Doris Lindner produced by Worcester Royal Porcelain Co., 1968, in a limited edition of 500

30 *Victorian Lady Models* by Ruth van Ruyckevelt produced by Worcester Royal Porcelain Co., 1968, in a limited edition of 500

Redstarts modelled by Dorothy Doughty produced by Worcester Royal
Porcelain Co., 1968, in a limited edition of 500

2 *HRH The Duke of Edinburgh*
modelled by Doris Lindner
produced by Worcester
Royal Porcelain Co., 1968,
in a limited edition of 750

3 North American Indian
designed by Peggy Davies
for Expo 67, produced by
Royal Doulton in a limited
edition of 500

34 *Below and opposite* (36)
Lounge chair and ottoman designed by Charles Eames for Herman Miller Inc., 1956

35 Wickerwork settee designed by Michael Thonet,
    c. 1851

37 Sussex chair, based on a traditional country type made by Morris and Co., 1866

Below

38 Left: Steel wire chair designed by Harry Bertoia for Knoll Associates Inc, New York, 1950

39 Right: Armchair, designed by le Corbusier, Pierre Jeanneret and Charlotte Perriand, 1929; still in production

LEDA.

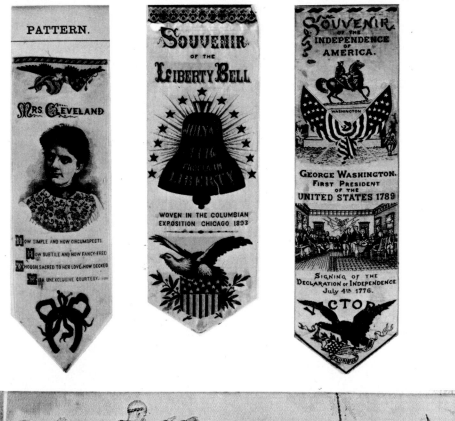

COLUMBUS LEAVING SPAIN 1492

WOVEN IN PURE SILK AT THE WORLD'S COLUMBIAN EXPOSITION, CHICAGO, 1893.

LANDING OF COLUMBUS OCT 12 1492

WOVEN IN PURE SILK AT THE WORLD'S COLUMBIAN EXPOSITION, CHICAGO, 1893.

43 Left: Edwardian fashion doll with wooden body, dressed in straw hat,
black damask dress, and black-and-white striped velvet jacket
Right: Large doll with jointed body; head with moving eyes and red hair,
c. 1860

44 Exhibition standard 2 in. scale model of the J & H McLaren DCC three-speed, four-shaft road haulage locomotive 'Henry V' built by J. Bevan of Monmouth

46   Model stable dated 1936

47   Rare, $\frac{1}{8}$ in. scale working model of HMS *Tiger*

48 1910 Rolls Royce 'Silver Ghost' tourer

49 1910 Humber

Opposite

51 Queen's Ware mug, one of six commemorative pieces made by Wedgwood for the
investiture of HRH Prince Charles as the
Prince of Wales

50 Mayflower Plate, produced in a limited
edition of 2500. Specially commissioned by
the Sutton Harbour Improvement Co to
mark the 350th anniversary of the *Mayflower's* departure

52 Spode china plate, one of limited edition of 5000 commissioned by Thomas
Goode & Co to mark the second anniversary of Sir Winston Churchill's
death. *Right:* Reproduction of the special back stamp printed in fine gold
within the foot of the plate

classes in Britain, even during the lengthy periods in the eighteenth century when Britain and France were at war with each other. The Empire styles of the mid-nineteenth century were extremely popular in Britain, and even to this day a considerable quantity of Empire furniture remains, despite the fact that a tremendous amount of it has been exported to the United States since the Second World War. Furniture from Switzerland and Belgium was also imported into Britain in the latter half of the nineteenth century, and much of that which has survived is of interest to the collector because of its relatively simple lines. It is interesting to note that the earliest record of Scandinavian furniture being sold in England appeared in 1867. Princess (later Queen) Alexandra helped to popularize Danish furniture in mid-Victorian England, though this was a far cry from the austerely elegant styles imported from Sweden and Finland in ensuing decades. Nor should the influence of the British Empire itself be overlooked. Centuries of commercial and social intercourse with India and the Far East had a direct influence on the furniture fashions of Victorian England. Following the acquisition of Hong Kong in 1841 and the opening up of British trade with China, Oriental furniture, both genuine and imitation, became increasingly popular. As the century wore on, English furniture became more and more eclectic— borrowing indiscriminately from the styles of past eras and other countries. The results were often unfortunate. As a rule the typical late-Victorian furniture was heavy, over-ornamented and fussy to a degree. The pomposity of its carving and scrollwork has often been ridiculed by succeeding generations and has little aesthetic appeal nowadays. Here and there, however, there are pieces which do not conform to the usual concept of Victorian furniture; these types now have a definite following and, consequently, a market value today. Some of the following types are worth looking out for.

PAPIER-MÂCHÉ

The use of a paper composition in the manufacture of furniture and furnishings seems to have been fairly well established in Britain by the mid-eighteenth century. It is alluded to in *Chambers' Encyclopaedia*, 1753, and at that time papier-mâché was used in picture frames, ceiling ornament and fine embossed work on furniture. This was regarded as a cheap substitute for stucco or even for the intricate carving found on the edges of tables or the backs of chairs. By the end of the eighteenth century there were firms in London specializing in the production of papier-mâché mouldings

I

which were then bought by furniture-makers all over the country and used to finish the appearance of their own products. The papier-mâché used for this purpose corresponds to the substance known by this name today and consists essentially of paper pulp which has been poured into moulds in the liquid state and then allowed to dry out.

To the Victorians, however, the term meant something rather different where furniture was concerned. In 1772 Henry Clay invented a process for making boards out of sheets of paper which were pasted together in layers and compressed under great force to form a hard, durable, yet extremely light substance. Clay distinguished between true papier-mâché and his own product by calling it 'paper ware', and the articles he made from it were known by this term for many years. This paper board resembled wood in many respects: it could be cut and sawn, planed and smoothed. It was then given a most attractive surface by the application of lacquer (japanning) and finished off with a high polish which gave it a brilliant lustre.

Paper ware was regarded as something of a curiosity, and it di not quite catch on with the public until the 1840s when the Birmingham firm of Jennens and Bettridge popularized it, primarily for small, light articles, such as tea trays, cake stands and writing cases, which lent themselves effectively to this medium. Hitherto tea trays had been made of sheet metal which was then japanned by hand. Not only were the paper trays lighter and more convenient but this material was more acceptable to the japanners, who found it capable of a more satisfying and lustrous finish. Jennens and Bettridge did not distinguish between Clay's sheet process and the more traditional moulded pulp process and referred to both indiscriminately as papier-mâché. Thus beginners are often surprised to learn that the tough light-weight trays with their brilliant black gloss surface are, in fact, papier-mâché.

It was not long before Jennens and Bettridge began to experiment with more ambitious articles in papier-mâché. Chairs and tables, judiciously reinforced with steel rods, were followed by cabinets, bookcases, wardrobes and even bedsteads in japanned papier-mâché. The material was strong and light, but the manufacturers tended to get carried away with the novelty of using it. Instead of designing articles to suit the best qualities of the material, they often produced typically Victorian furniture, elaborately decorated, in papier-mâché. Well might Richard Redgrave, commenting on the paper ware displayed by Jennens and Bettridge at the Great Exhibition, describe it as 'a mass of barbarous splendour that offends the eye and quarrels with every

130

other kind of manufacture with which it comes in contact'. Where the lines of the piece were kept as simple as possible, however, papier-mâché was most effective; it is these objects which are now most highly sought after.

The decoration on papier-mâché furniture varied considerably. An effective form of ornament consisted of gilding, which contrasted most attractively with the glossy black surface. Joseph Booth was employed by Jennens and Bettridge to decorate papier-mâché furniture in the chinoiserie styles which had long been popular on japanned furniture manufactured in more conventional materials. Booth's intricate floral and Oriental decoration stands out from that of his successors and imitators. As papier-mâché ware increased in popularity, however, ornamentation became more mechanical. Decoration was often stencilled on to the surface, and the composition of the gilding (originally in gold leaf or gold powder) was debased into powdered alloys of copper and zinc, which might have looked like the real thing when new, but which tarnished badly with the passage of time.

Highly prized nowadays are examples of papier-mâché furniture with pearl inlay work. As early as 1825 George Souter, who was also employed by Jennens and Bettridge, perfected a technique of inlaying thin pieces of pearl shell on papier-mâché and then painting them with varnish. When this was dry, a coat of acid was applied. The unvarnished portions of the shell were eaten away by the acid, leaving the varnished areas in a pleasing design. As well as pearl shell various semi-precious stones or glass paste gems were used for inlay work on japanned papier-mâché. Coloured prints were also stuck on papier-mâché and then varnished over. Floral and scenic decoration became increasingly elaborate, and at the zenith of papier-mâché ware (1860–70) it seemed that one could never have too much of a good thing. In the ensuing decades, however, the very exuberance of the decoration on late papier-mâché ware proved its undoing, and by the end of the century it had gone completely out of fashion. It is only within the past ten years that there has been a revival of interest in Victorian papier-mâché wares, and prices—virtually non-existent in 1955—have trebled for the better-quality pieces since 1965. Collectors are particularly keen on items with the name of Jennens and Bettridge impressed on them, but there were many other firms who cashed in on the popularity of this medium, and their products are often far from inferior. The larger items are not very plentiful nowadays, but since they are comparatively unpopular with collectors anyway, they are not particularly expensive. There is, however, a great demand for the smaller decorative objects such as fire screens, music racks and stands, occasional tables, work boxes and writing cases, and these now fetch sums up to £100 ($240) or more, depending on condition and quality.

One of the reasons for the popularity of papier-mâché furniture in the 1860s and 1870s in Britain was the craze at that time for anything Japanese in appearance. For fifteen years or so before the Meiji Restoration of 1868 Japan had been opened up to trade with America and Europe, and while this resulted in the deplorable Westernization of Japan, the traffic was not by any means all in one direction. Another manifestation of the Japanese 'craze' was the enormous popularity of flimsy bamboo furniture, which reached its height by the mid-1870s. Everywhere one found examples of bamboo furniture: tables, chairs, cabinets, what-nots, lamps and even bedsteads. This material was particularly suited to bedroom furniture, but in its heyday it was also used for drawing-room pieces—tables and sideboards. Bamboo furniture was economical, since the basic materials were cheap and the methods of construction relatively straightforward. It was often combined with fine basket or cane work, and sometimes used in conjunction with wood (e.g. table tops and the panels in desks and cabinets). The result was often light and pleasing and surprisingly strong. Although the vogue for this furniture declined towards the end of the century, it never quite died out. Within the past few years it has returned to favour and, while not quite strong enough to be a commercial proposition, it has caught the fancy of the collector; thus pieces which a few years ago were quite unsaleable now have a definite market value. Originally the bamboo was left in its natural honey-brown state, but in the revival of interest it is fashionable to paint it, either white or in a strong colour such as red.

BUHL AND MARQUETRY

Buhl (sometimes written as Boulle) is a term used to denote a particular form of inlay work in which brass was inlaid on tortoiseshell or vice versa. Thin veneers of Buhl work were used in the decoration of panels on commodes, sideboards and tables of all kinds. Despite its German-sounding name, this technique was, in fact, brought to Britain from France, and many of the workers employed in this side of the furniture industry in Britain were Frenchmen. When executed properly Buhl work presented an attractive, smooth surface capable of taking a high polish. Collectors are especially interested in examples in which the brass inlay has been intricately engraved.

Marquetry, too, was introduced to England from France, where it had been practised in the furniture trade for generations. Part of the attraction of fine eighteenth-century French furniture lay in its intricate marquetry panelling. In the mid-nineteenth century French marquetry-cutters settled in England and catered to a growing demand for this form of decoration. Increasing use was made of exotic timbers from America, Asia and Africa for the thin sheets of veneer used in marquetry, and an astonishingly colourful array of different veneers were eventually employed to give the most varied results. During the last third of the century the English furniture trade developed a high reputation for fine marquetry, even capturing many export orders which the French market lost after the disastrous Franco-Prussian War of 1870.

True marquetry was a painstaking process requiring great skill and patience on the part of the cutter. Each piece of veneer had to be sawn carefully to the exact dimensions required, and considerable care was taken to match the various pieces to achieve the proper harmony of shades and textures. The pieces were assembled like a jigsaw puzzle to form the desired pattern or picture and then glued to the panel or table top. The marquetry surface was skilfully polished to present a smooth, level appearance. Like everything else, however, as the Victorian era wore on, quality and appearance in marquetry were sacrificed in attempts to cut labour costs: a cheap method of producing a kind of marquetry was evolved in the 1870s. In this process the marquetry was stamped out on a mass production basis instead of being hand-sawn or cut as before. This could be achieved by using much thinner veneers, so that, while the initial appearance of these instant marquetry panels was fairly satisfactory, they did not possess the same durability and tended to crack or peel off. The collector is advised, therefore, to exercise great care in the purchase of Victorian marquetry. The best is comparable to anything produced in France in the eighteenth century, but too much of the later material was cheap and shoddy at the time of its manufacture and, unfortunately, has not aged gracefully.

IRON

Wrought iron has been recorded as a constituent of furniture from the late Middle Ages onwards, usually well concealed with upholstery and fabric coverings. The British vogue for iron as such, for use in gardens and on patios, did not emerge until the eighteenth century, and remained of modest proportions until the Victorians evolved cheap and economic methods of producing such furniture, not in wrought iron but in cast iron. Vast quantities of benches, chairs and tables, primarily intended for outdoor use, were produced in cast iron. Nowadays it is customary to paint iron furniture (usually in black or white), mainly to protect it from the corrosive effects of wind and rain. The Victorians, however, painted their iron furniture in attempts to simulate the appearance of wood or stone. Elaborate techniques were devised to produce the graining in wood or the delicate veining of fine marble; it is difficult to understand, at this remove, why the Victorians should have taken such pride in painting iron furniture to make it look like something else. Present-day taste accepts the elaborate scrollwork and decoration on Victorian cast iron, but only if the ornamentation is relieved by the use of pure white or black paint.

It is difficult to summarize the various aspects of Victorian furniture within the scope of a short chapter, but it would be unfair and incorrect to dismiss the furniture of the greater part of the nineteenth century as unworthy of the collector's serious interest. It is unfortunate that the nadir of English furniture design should have coincided with the Great Exhibition of 1851, since the publicity given to the exhibits displayed there had a marked influence on public taste for the rest of the century, both in Britain and in America. On the other hand, the sixty-four years of Victoria's reign was a very long time, and it would be not only surprising, but an indictment of public taste, were something better not to have emerged during that period.

A revolt against the florid over-ornamentation of the mid-Victorian period resulted in the development, in the 1860s, of a new style in furniture design known deceptively as 'Early English'. The appearance of this style coincided with the great Paris Exposition of 1867, where it was first shown to the public to any appreciable degree, and it had an immediate impact on the fashionable world. This was reinforced and sustained by the publication the following year of *Hints on Household Taste* by Charles Locke Eastlake. This book enjoyed a wide circulation on both sides of the Atlantic and dominated the outlook on furniture styles in Britain and America up to the time of the First World War. An early exponent of the Early English style was William Morris, who regarded its simple lines as conducive to good craftsmanship. His sound, common-sense views on what constituted good furniture were stated in his *Lesser Arts of Life*:

134

'Our furniture should be good citizens' furniture, solid and well made in workmanship, and in design should have nothing about it that is not easily defensible, no monstrosities or extravagances, not even of beauty, lest we weary of it. As to matters of construction, it should not have to depend on the special skill of a very picked workman, or the super-excellence of his glue, but be made on the proper principles of the art of joinery; also I think that, except for very movable things like chairs, it should not be so very light as to be nearly imponderable; it should be made of timber rather than walking-sticks.'

The so-called Early English style of furniture attempted to break away from the ponderous and elaborate pieces, the massive sideboards and hideous overmantels of the period. It was—Morris notwithstanding—fairly light and extremely elegant in the main. Curves were kept to a minimum, and the accent was placed on straight lines in a rectangular form. This was the direct antithesis of the typically mid-Victorian delight in curved backs and legs on chairs, elaborately shaped sideboards and ubiquitous scrollwork. Eastlake condemned this in *Hints on Household Taste*, saying, 'Chairs are invariably curved in such a manner as to ensure the greatest amount of ugliness with the least possible comfort.'

In the last two decades of the century a type of furniture developed in Britain known as Art Furniture. It was given this name because its producers, firms such as Morris, Heal and Liberty, were consciously striving to produce something which had a highly aesthetic appeal. To achieve this they employed de-signers, artists and architects with established reputations in this or related fields. Typical of the men who turned their consider-able talents to furniture design at this time were Bruce Talbert, William Burges, Philip Webb and John S. Chapple, and pieces identifiable as their work now have quite a high market value. One of the best known and most prolific of the Art Furniture de-signers was Christopher Dresser, a lecturer in botany by profes-sion, who was deeply influenced by the art of Japan following a visit to that country in 1876. He was responsible for the growth of the cult of Japanese styles in furniture in the later years of the century, as the Early English style began to decline. There was also the renaissance of Chippendale, Sheraton, Adam and Hepplewhite designs which, beginning in the late 1870s, has con-tinued, off and on, down to the present day. So-called 'Queen Anne' and 'Gothic' styles also enjoyed a measure of popularity in the closing years of the nineteenth century, but both were overshadowed by the tremendous influence of the Art Nouveau movement which dominated the applied arts as much as it did the fine arts in the period up to the outbreak of the First World War.

Despite its French name, Art Nouveau had its origins in England as far as furniture was concerned (in the field of glassware, however, it originated with Louis Tiffany in the United States). Art Nouveau furniture was distinguished by its use of naturalistic forms—tendrils, foliage, branches and roots of trees were popular motifs. Long, trailing ivy or tulip motifs were used to decorate tables and chair backs, either painted on to the surface or inlaid in contrasting woods. Another popular device consisted of applying the decoration in metalwork. Copper, brass and pewter were the favourite materials, though silver is not uncommon. Not only the decoration but the shape of the furniture was characterized by sinuous, undulating lines. Unfortunately, however, these lines and curves, ideal perhaps for ceramic and silver decoration, did not lend themselves too well to furniture design. Because it was at its least successful in furniture, the recent revival of interest in Art Nouveau in general has not applied to material in this field to any great extent. One of the principal exponents of the Art Nouveau style in furniture was the architect Charles Rennie Macintosh. He is best remembered today for his tall, narrow, perpendicular lines, which may have been eminently suited to the Glasgow School of Art which he designed, but which were quite ludicrous and uncomfortable when applied to the design of chair backs. Macintosh's furniture possesses a certain academic value these days, as an interesting facet of the work produced by this versatile architect, but the same cannot be said of the furniture designed by his successors and imitators. Art Nouveau furniture failed ultimately because it ignored traditional forms and elements in furniture design. Cabinet-work became imbued with extravagance and a startling lack of realism in the absurd quest for originality. Inevitably the decline set in within ten years of its inception. If we mark the beginning of Art Nouveau with S. Bing's opening of his Paris boutique 'La Maison de l'Art Nouveau' in 1894, then, by 1905, the movement was certainly on its way out.

It is interesting to note a parallel development in the United States about the same period. Oak furniture in the so-called Mission style, popular at the end of the nineteenth century, was supposed to be a return to the simplicity believed to be characteristic of the Spanish Mission furniture and architecture of old California. In reality, however, this furniture bore little resemblance to the Spanish Mission period, being a purely American manifestation of the Art Nouveau style then sweeping Europe. Mission furniture has, however, worn better than its European counterpart, and the demand for it today is steady in the United

States, where a certain degree of nostalgia (real or imagined) for the good old days has assured it a measure of popularity.

Although we may ridicule the strange appearance of the furniture produced as a result of the various crazes which dominated the last quarter of the nineteenth century, at least we can give the designers credit for striving to break free from the hideously over-ornamented, solid furniture of the High Victorian era. The fumblings and tentative gropings of Talbert, Lethaby, Macintosh and others, so often despised nowadays, marked the beginning of the search for simplicity and functionalism which have both been realized in the best of modern furniture. The Arts and Crafts movement of the 1880s led the way, and if Art Nouveau may be regarded as an aberration in this development, by the beginning of the present century the ideals of simplicity and functionalism at the expense of ornamentation were making themselves felt. This movement began in the United States, where the architects Frank Lloyd Wright and Louis Sullivan were the first to lay down the principle that form should follow function. These ideals were adopted and greatly expanded in Germany, first of all by the Deutsche Werkbund (founded in 1907) and then, after the First World War, by a Werkbund member, Walter Gropius, who founded the Bauhaus at Weimar. In 1925 the Bauhaus moved to Dessau, and it was from there that the Bauhaus movement exerted its greatest influence on architecture and furniture design all over the world. The effects of the Bauhaus principles of a creative approach to architecture are still being felt. Many of the ideas on functional design which are now universally accepted were born at Dessau in the late 1920s, and the advent of National Socialism in 1933, which forced Gropius and his associates to leave Germany, merely helped to speed up the dissemination of these ideas in other parts of Europe and, most of all, in America. In some respects the Bauhaus disciples went too far in their rejection of ornament, and much of the avant-garde furniture of the 1930s has been criticized as featureless, sterile and monotonous.

Fortunately the worst excesses of functionalism were tempered by the work of designers who possessed an intimate knowledge of traditional styles. A thorough grounding in the work of their predecessors has been found essential to the good furniture designers of today: the basic principles of good design and proportion simply cannot be ignored. Thus the tendency nowadays is to borrow the best ideas from the work of Chippendale, Adams, Sheraton and

Hepplewhite, amalgamate them with the finest aspects of furniture design from other periods and other parts of the world (from classical Chinese to French rococo) and to adapt them to contemporary needs. It is heartening to note that the best of modern furniture has succeeded in incorporating features of traditional forms and, while obeying the dictates of simplicity and functionalism, has rejected the worst excesses and bizarre conceptions of the 1920s and 1930s. Good modern furniture is designed on the principles of utilitarianism and a simple beauty—which are not, after all, incompatible.

Since the Second World War it is encouraging to note that the standards of design and workmanship in furniture have risen considerably. This is partly due to the growth in recent years of colleges and art schools specializing in furniture design and manufacture, and partly due to the development of public bodies (such as the Council of Industrial Design in Britain) whose conscious aim is to improve and maintain standards of design and workmanship. The public, who buy and use furniture, are also far more discriminating and sophisticated than their predecessors. The new bourgeoisie of the Victorian era and even the *nouveaux riches* of the 1920s lacked the background, breeding and innate good taste which distinguished the upper classes of the eighteenth century. Better general education, higher levels of prosperity and a more universal awareness of all that constitutes the best quality in furniture mark out the present generation, so that manufacturers have the stimulus and incentive to continue producing work of a high order.

Looking back over the past hundred years or so, in England, and endeavouring to pick out the most enduring and most worthwhile furniture, I should single out the work of such men as Sir Ambrose Heal, who combined the qualities of a first-rate craftsman with the originality and genius of the true artist. His designs for both hand-made and machine-made furniture have had a far-reaching influence on present-day trends. In the same category I would place Sir Gordon Russell, who established a family furniture business in the Cotswold village of Broadway where fine-quality furniture is produced to this day. Ernest Gimson's workshops at Daneway House have been responsible for numerous fine pieces of furniture in the past seventy years. The remarkable Barnsleys—brothers Ernest and Sidney and the latter's son Edward—have produced fine work of individual craftsmanship. The late Arthur B. Reynolds, who worked for many years with Stanley Davis of Windermere, founded the business at Ludlow, Shropshire, which is carried on to this day by his two sons.

Reynolds of Ludlow are renowned for their excellent furniture in traditional English styles, in walnut, oak, yew, cherry and other age-old materials.

These businesses have produced machine-made and hand-made furniture of a uniform excellence. There are, however, a vast number of artist-craftsmen working in small units and operating largely by hand in the production of top-quality furniture in individual designs. These wood-workers, many of them little known outside their own locality, include full-time professionals, artists whose work extends into other fields and teachers at art schools and colleges. The common denominator which qualifies their work is their sheer love of the materials which they use, the creative genius and high degree of technical competence which they bring to bear on their work. In a sense they have recaptured the old atmosphere of the cabinet-makers and designers who laboured in those palmy days before the Industrial Revolution brought such radical changes in furniture-making.

During the past decade furniture has become more 'international' and increasingly eclectic, drawing on the best from former styles, from op and pop art, from the Edwardian and Victorian periods and showing a marked African or Asian influence. Add to this a dash of Bauhaus and a sprinkling of Art Deco and the result is a style which is all of these and yet unlike any one of them. For the first time also the two radically different approaches to furniture design have been happily blended. The 'structural' approach, involving the use of tubular steel and plastics, is combined with the more traditional approach using age-old materials such as leather and wood. Increasing use has been made of glass-fibre and plastics to create the sculptured forms associated predominantly with Scandinavian design and with the famous chair shapes created by such designers as Harry Bertoia, Arne Jacobsen and Eero Saarinen.

At the present time the best designed furniture comes from Britain, the Netherlands, West Germany, Italy and the Scandinavian countries, but there is little to distinguish the country of origin in such work. In many respects the work of the designers mentioned above is still in advance of public taste and too expensive for the mass market; yet their influence is now much in evidence even in the more conventional work produced for the domestic market. Prototypes such as the Bertoia chair may safely be regarded as antiques of the future—so far as any modern furniture may be considered in this light. However, much of the furniture being produced today is almost clinical in appearance and lacks the aesthetic appeal of previous styles. Whether this furniture will be highly regarded in years to come merely on academic, stylistic grounds or will arouse a genuine demand in accordance with a radical change in public taste, can only be conjectured.

This brings us back to the point at which this chapter began. Is it fair to regard 1830 as the year in which good furniture design and manufacture came to an end? Despite the vicissitudes of the industry in the past century and a half, I should like to think that there have been sufficient oases of good design in the wilderness of mass produced shoddy goods and tastelessness to answer that question in the negative. Today, however, the efforts of the Council of Industrial Design, the Crafts Centre of Great Britain, the Red Rose Guild of Craftsmen, the Arts Council of Great Britain, the Rural Industries Bureau and similar bodies have led to a dramatic reversal in the fortunes of furniture making. The trend of the past 140 years has been reversed, and the industry has been turned into a craft once more.

7 Woven silk pictures

The city of Coventry has been famous for its textile industry for more than three centuries, ever since the French Huguenot refugees came to England, bringing their trades and professions with them. The silk weavers settled in the Midlands and established a flourishing industry based on Coventry. The bulk of their output consisted of silk ribbons, which were extremely fashionable until the middle of the nineteenth century. At its zenith the industry supported thousands of workers, and the development of the Jacquard loom in the 1830s made it possible to weave multi-coloured, patterned designs on an automatic basis. Silk ribbons with gaudy, exuberant pictorial motifs were displayed at the Great Exhibition of 1851, but they failed to find favour with the judges, who considered them in bad taste. The picture ribbons were, however, avidly purchased by the general public, and for a brief period they enjoyed tremendous popularity. After the trade agreements with France in the late 1850s and 1860s the English market was flooded with cheaper foreign ribbons, and the Coventry silk industry, faced with such unequal competition, went into rapid decline.

It was in 1854, shortly before this decline began, that Thomas Stevens became established in Coventry as a manufacturer of silk ribbons. Stevens had the perspicacity to recognize the growing problems of the British ribbon industry and the genius to convert his factory to something more profitable. Instead of ribbons he began to produce silk woven bookmarks, adapting his looms and equipment to manufacture a continuous ribbon woven with a repeated motif which could then be cut up into the requisite lengths and tipped with tassels. The bookmarks produced by Stevens were usually either Biblical or literary, with suitable religious texts on the one hand or quotations from the great masters of English literature on the other. These silk bookmarks were a popular form of prize in schools and Sunday schools in the mid-Victorian period but relatively few of them have survived. There is no great demand for them, however, and they can usually be picked up for a few shillings at most. Stevens also produced bookmarks featuring early locomotives or balloons, and these are now in great demand by collectors of miscellanea connected with the history of transport.

At the International Exhibition of 1862 Stevens had a machine on display, giving working demonstrations of the weaving of these silk bookmarks. They were highly successful, at a time when the silk textile industry in England was being hard hit by foreign competition. Some idea of their success may be gained from the fact that his trade catalogue of 1875 listed no fewer than five hundred different subjects reproduced on woven silk bookmarks. Not content with this, Stevens soon turned to other media for his silk woven pictures, producing silk calendars, Christmas cards, Valentines, lavender sachets, decorated hat bands and emblematical sashes. With the exception of the greetings cards there is little interest shown in, or demand for, the other categories today; although, as Victoriana, they are beginning to excite the curiosity of collectors generally.

But the object for which Stevens became famous in his lifetime, and which has since been immortalized by collectors, was the Stevengraph or woven silk picture produced as an ornament *per se*. Stevens successfully adapted the Jacquard loom in the early 1870s so that it could produce a comparatively large picture in anything up to a dozen colours. It is not known for certain when he first began to produce these Stevengraphs, but they had become so successful by 1876 that he had built new premises in Coventry and given his factory the grandiose title of the Stevengraph Works. At the York Exhibition in 1879 one of the most popular attractions was the public demonstration of silk picture weaving given by Stevens. The silk pictures, usually measuring about six inches by two inches, sold for sixpence or a shilling (eighteenpence if mounted and glazed), and they were evidently sold by the thousand to the sightseers at the Exhibition, judging by the large number of York Exhibition Stevengraphs which have survived to this day. They were mostly bought as decorative souvenirs of the occasion, though the Earl of Shrewsbury is recorded as having purchased one as a present for his butler!

Technically speaking, the best of the Stevengraphs are superb examples of ingenuity and simple artistry. The colouring was usually vigorous, without being garish, and great attention was lavished on small details such as the shading on clothing and figures in order to impart a three-dimensional effect. This was also achieved in background and foreground scenery by the

142

cunning variation of texture and closeness in the weaving. The composition of such spirited action scenes as 'The Boat Race' and 'The Last Lap' is carefully contrived in such a way that the backgrounds are carefully delineated down to the minutest detail without detracting from the main subject of the design. Generally, the backgrounds were produced in muted colours and soft, pale shades, whereas the foreground detail was picked out in bright, vivid colours. The different stitches and patterns employed to build up the detail of a picture indicate the astonishing virtuosity of the Jacquard loom in the hands of a competent craftsman. Though Stevens had his imitators, few of them were able to equal him, and none surpassed him in the delicacy and subtlety with which his silk pictures were woven. To appreciate this fully, it is necessary to study Stevengraphs under a good magnifying glass; then one can see how sensitively the features of people, even those in the background, are delineated, and appreciate the incredibly intricate set-up of complex subjects such as the spokes of bicycle wheels (in 'The Last Lap'). The composition of Stevengraphs, though simple, is singularly effective, vividly capturing the elements of movement, especially in the racing scenes. It is small wonder, therefore, that the Stevengraph should have been so popular in its heyday and that although the Stevengraph Works has long been a thing of the past, these charming silk pictures are so avidly collected today.

Stevengraphs fall into a number of clear-cut categories, some of which are more eagerly sought after than others. One of the largest categories is the sporting scene. Bearing in mind the English propensity for sport of all kinds, it is hardly surprising that this subject should loom so large. This category can be further subdivided into horse racing subjects, hunting scenes, the boat races, cricket, boxing and cycling. The horse racing Stevengraphs often portrayed famous contemporary jockeys, in a bewildering array of different racing colours. The great Fred Archer, for example, is shown in the colours of either the Prince of Wales, the Duke of Westminster, Lord Falmouth, Mr Mantar, Mr Peck or Mr T. Jennings, Jr. Among the most popular versions of the Fred Archer Stevengraph is the one which shows him mounted on Iroquois. Other popular jockeys who were a continual source of inspiration to Stevens included F. Barratt, Tom Cannon, John Osborne and C. Wood. Among the steeple-chasing scenes were favourites such as 'The Start', 'The Water Jump' and 'The Finish'. Indeed, it is true to say that these Stevengraphs, and the hunting series (which included 'Full Cry' and 'The Kill'), were the poor man's Alken prints—though nowadays there may be little monetary differential between the finest Stevengraphs and the usual run of Alken prints.

The boxing scenes either depicted famous matches or portrayed such celebrated pugilists as John L. Sullivan and 'Gentleman Jim' Corbett. The cricket Stevengraphs featured general scenes from the game, but an unusual (and now quite rare) one bore a full-length portrait of Dr W.G. Grace, the outstanding nineteenth-century batsman. A fine example of the latter, incidentally, made £145 ($348) in a Knight, Frank and Rutley sale in March 1968; this was quite a high price at that time, though it has since been reduced to comparative insignificance by those obtained for certain Stevengraphs at more recent sales. The Oxford–Cambridge Boat Race was of perennial topicality and consequently inspired quite a variety of Stevengraphs. These are particularly prized in sets, with the captions 'Are You Ready', 'The Final Spurt' and 'The Finish'.

Another category of Stevengraphs is that showing mechanical devices connected with transport in one form or another. These include the highly popular coaching Stevengraphs, showing 'The London and York Royal Mail Coach', for example, or various locomotives entitled 'Stephenson's Triumph', 'The First Train' or 'The Present Time—60 Miles an Hour'. The locomotive Stevengraphs are of absorbing interest to railway enthusiasts and are eagerly sought after in all their many, subtle variations. The pictures entitled 'The Present Time', for example, may be found with two or two and a half carriages, or a comparatively modern express train with six or eight coaches, or may show a train coming from under a bridge and so on. The early versions of 'The Present Time' are now worth a great deal of money—from £40 ($96) to £100 ($240) having been paid for the scarcer varieties. Surprisingly enough, there are even Stevengraphs with early aeronautical subjects. Most of them show balloon ascents—a reminder of the popularity of ballooning in the late nineteenth century—but a few are also recorded with vintage aeroplanes, and these are in great demand with aviation enthusiasts nowadays.

Under the heading of popular heroism may be included such Stevengraphs as those commemorating the redoubtable Grace Darling, whose courage enabled the rescue of shipwrecked seamen off the Farne Islands in 1838. The dramatic pictures entitled 'Called to the Rescue' featured a lifeboat battling through stormy seas. Another item in the same *genre* depicted a fire engine drawn by dashing horses. Time and time again the equestrian theme is found in Stevengraphs, testifying to the enduring popularity of horses in nineteenth-century England in all strata of society.

Inevitably one of the most popular subjects of this sort concerns Lady Godiva, whose procession in the nude through the city of Coventry saved its citizens from further excessive taxation by her husband, Leofric of Mercia. Therle Hughes, in *More Small Decorative Antiques*, has identified the source of one series of Godiva Stevengraphs as an engraving by D. Jee in Withington's *English Pageantry*, volume II, but there were numerous versions of the Godiva theme which were probably quite original to Stevens. The series usually consists of 'Ye Ladye Godiva', 'Ye Peeping Tom of Coventre' and a view of the procession itself. The Godiva motif was one of the most popular subjects for Stevengraphs and was used right down to 1940, when the Blitz on Coventry put an untimely end to the Stevengraph Works. 'Dick Turpin's Ride to York, on his bonnie Black Bess, 1739' was another popular equestrian subject, found in a variety of designs.

Religious and mythological subjects form two more important categories. The Biblical scenes were an elaboration of, and direct descendant of, the Sunday school bookmarks, but the mythological Stevengraphs represented the best attempt to raise the silk woven picture into the realm of pure art and, indeed, it is the finest of these classical studies which are the most highly regarded Stevengraphs today. At auctions of Stevengraphs in 1968, for example, 'Phoebus and Aurora' was sold for £75 ($180) and 'The Bath of Psyche' made £60 ($144). The most expensive of the classical Stevengraphs, however, is 'Leda and the Swan', which, at £120 ($288), established a new record price for Stevengraphs at Knight, Frank and Rutley's sale in March 1968. The same silk reached a similar price in a further sale in June 1968, but this apparently large sum paled into insignificance in October 1968 when an exceptionally fine example of 'Leda' was sold at Knight, Frank and Rutley for £460 ($1104).

Portraits form a very large group of Stevengraphs. In many respects they were the two-dimensional equivalent of the Staffordshire pottery figures which also served to commemorate the great celebrities of the nineteenth century. Queen Victoria and Prince Albert were, inevitably, the most popular subjects. The portraits of the Queen were numerous, and varied from studies of her as a young woman, based on Winterhalter's famous painting of 1846, to the serenely dignified portrait used on the Stevengraphs produced at the time of the Golden Jubilee in 1887. Contemporary European royalty were similarly favoured, from the Tsar of Russia to the venerable Franz Josef of Austria and the young Kaiser Wilhelm II of Germany. Comparatively scarce are the Stevengraphs portraying Napoleon III, Emperor of the French,

K   145 since he was deposed in 1870, and only the earliest series bore his portrait. British politicians include the Prime Minister, W.E. Gladstone, and popular figures of the period such as Joseph Chamberlain, John Bright and the Irish Nationalist leader Charles Stuart Parnell. An interesting Stevengraph, combining royalty with politics, shows Queen Victoria surrounded by her various Prime Ministers. An exceptionally fine example of this Stevengraph was sold in 1968 for £62 ($149). Other portrait silks showed literary figures such as Robert Burns (sold for £125 ($300) in 1968), historic personages such as William of Orange—a popular subject with Ulster Protestants—and popular heroes and heroines such as Grace Darling and Buffalo Bill.

Feats of engineering were the subject of many Stevengraphs, among which may be mentioned the Forth Bridge, the Old Tyne Bridge, the Clifton Suspension Bridge and the Mersey Tunnel. Stevens was fully aware of the propaganda value of international trade fairs and exhibitions and, as well as supporting them, he wove silk souvenirs of these occasions. Besides the York Exhibition of 1879, Stevengraphs may be found commemorating the exhibitions in Glasgow and Edinburgh, the Exposition Universelle d'Anvers of 1898 and the Columbian Exposition of 1893.

For the last-mentioned exhibition Stevens produced a series of rare American silk pictures which, on account of their scarcity and the great demand for them in the United States today, fetch very high prices in good condition. Among the most desirable are those showing the signing of the Declaration of Independence, Washington crossing the Delaware and Christopher Columbus, all of which rate over £100 ($240) nowadays. The scope of Stevengraph collecting is enormous, and their value ranges from a pound or two to several hundreds.

The value of a Stevengraph depends not only on the subject depicted and on its condition but also on the date of issue. Since very few actually bear a date in their inscription, this has to be ascertained by other means. Stevengraphs are invariably mounted on a light green or fawn-coloured mat with bevelled gilt openings. The card usually measures eight by five inches and, as well as bearing the title of the picture, it usually has an inscription relating to its manufacture. Thus an early picture might bear the legend 'Woven in pure silk' immediately beneath the picture. The usual inscription, used during the heyday of the Stevengraph read: 'Woven in silk by Thomas Stevens, inventor and manufacturer, Coventry and London (registered)', while latterly—in the early years of this century—the inscription was altered to 'Woven in silk by Thomas Stevens (Coventry) Ltd'.

146

Stevengraphs were either sold mounted on cards or were framed and glazed in a black wooden frame for an additional sixpence. The original mounting has a very important bearing on the value of a Stevengraph, especially since it should bear a label whose inscription is useful in dating the picture more precisely. Stevens regarded this label as a form of advertising, so it was used to list some of the other titles available. A single-title label, being one of the earliest, is the most desirable. Later Stevengraphs will be found with labels listing six or more pictures, and up to a dozen titles on one label are recorded. Between 1879 and 1883 Stevengraphs often bore on their label the diamond-shaped mark with a central 'Rd' indicating that the design had been registered at the Patent Office to protect it for three years from use by rival firms. The marginal letters and figures indicate registration at various times between 1879 and 1883 when this device was discontinued. Another clue is provided by the wording on the label; a reference to the various national and international medals awarded to Stevens is a good guide to the critical period of the 1870s and 1880s when the most valuable of the Stevengraphs were produced. The inclusion of a picture of the Stevengraph Works, for example, would date a silk after 1876. Incidentally, experts are divided over the question of whether the pictures gave their name to the factory or whether the name of the factory was subsequently transferred to the pictures. The word Stevengraph, used to denote a silk picture, is of comparatively recent acceptance, and the pictures were originally referred to as 'textilegraphs'.

The term 'Stevengraph', strictly speaking, applies only to the products of the Stevens factory; but it is now applied generically by collectors to any woven silk picture, although those actually manufactured and identified as Stevens' pictures command the highest prices. The other silk weaving companies were not slow to follow Stevens' example, and among the many rival firms whose work is collectable were W.H. Grant, J. Hart, Odell and French, J. Ratcliff & Son and the Silk Weaving Company of South Farnborough. The French weavers also imitated the Stevengraph, though usually in a much larger format, and of these the best known firm was Didier Petit. As a rule it is relatively easy to distinguish the products of the various factories, since they, too, usually labelled their silks; because of the increasing demand from collectors who place a premium on Stevens' silks, however, there has been a fair amount of forging of labels. The silk pictures of Thomas Stevens are reasonably well documented in two excellent monographs *The Silk Pictures of Thomas Stevens* by Wilma Baker and *Stevengraphs* by M.D. Darby, both of which list all the known varieties and give comprehensive explanations of the labels found on Stevengraphs.

The Stevengraph Works was still in production as late as 1940 when the Blitz on Coventry put an end to its activities. In the previous decades, however, interest in silk pictures had waned considerably, and although Stevengraphs were being produced up to 1940, they could only be regarded as a sideline to the company's main business of silk weaving. The vogue for Stevengraphs as wall decoration hardly survived the nineteenth century. The later examples, while comparatively rare, lack the detail, colouring and intricate weaving which distinguished the earlier pictures, and for these reasons they do not excite the same interest among collectors today.

Antiquarian interest in Stevengraphs began seriously in the United States before the Second World War, and the Stevengraph Collectors' Association, with headquarters at Irvington on Hudson, New York, was formed to encourage an intelligent appreciation of these charming pictures. In the land of their birth, however, very little interest was shown in them. The years between the two world wars marked the nadir of the Stevengraph. It is true that small woven silk pictures were produced in this period and given away with cigarette packets in lieu of the ubiquitous cigarette card, but somehow they failed to catch on with the public, and their relatively high cost of production made their use prohibitive. In recent years there have been several attempts to revive the woven silk picture as an art form, but with only limited success. This revival might have been possible when the silk weaving companies were producing similar items for utilitarian purposes, but since the garment industry now prefers a printed label instead of a woven silk one for stitching on to clothes, this aspect of the textile industry has rapidly declined. The biggest names in this field today are Cash, Brough & Nicholson and Franklins, all based in the Warwickshire–Staffordshire area. All three firms have produced limited editions of silk pictures, but seldom with an eye to commercial profit. The majority of these modern silks, such as Brough & Nicholson's fine reproduction of 'The Laughing Cavalier' or Franklin's sensitive rendering of Karsh's 'Angry Lion' portrait of the late Sir Winston Churchill, were produced more for prestige purposes than for commercial gain. As such, they are very difficult to find, but will undoubtedly deserve a place in any Stevengraph collection. Cash, best known for their woven name tapes and clothing labels, produced an interesting silk portrait of Lady Godiva in 1956, to mark the 900th anniversary of her famous ride. They have also produced an attractive reproduction in miniature of the Graham

148

Sutherland tapestry which now hangs in Coventry Cathedral, and this silk is, or was until recently, on sale at the Cathedral bookshop.

Franklins, formerly of Coventry and now based in Banbridge, Northern Ireland, produced an interesting series of six Shakespearean characters and a view of Shakespeare's birthplace to commemorate the quatercentenary of William Shakespeare in 1964. It is interesting to note that these modern Stevengraphs were woven in nylon fibre instead of the more traditional silk. The reason for this is that silk fibres, being rather short in the staple, are comparatively difficult to weave, and man-made yarn is more practicable. Of course nylon does not do the job as well as silk, and one cannot compare silk and nylon pictures for quality or the subtle nuances of which the former is capable. It is rather sad to think that silk weaving is a dying art, but perhaps in the future the woven nylon pictures of today will rival the Stevengraph for the attention of serious collectors. A novel adaptation of the woven picture consists of cards mounted with Stevengraphs as an ornamental vignette, space being left for an address and a stamp so that the card may be transmitted by post. Such modern Stevengraphs have recently appeared for use in conjunction with the special issues of postage stamps commemorating the maiden flight of Concorde and the Investiture of the Prince of Wales. These have been produced in very limited editions—not so much from deliberate choice but because the market for such mementoes is, at present, extremely small. Should this idea catch on, the modern Stevengraph would be assured of a bright future, but since the manufacturers are not really interested in this business, and since there has been little positive response from collectors so far, the fate of these interesting souvenirs is in the balance. The irony of it is that these items have at least an academic interest to the collector of silk pictures, and in view of the small quantities produced they are decidedly worth while purchasing now as possible antiques of the future.

8 The world in miniature

The fact that houses are much smaller today than was the case fifty or more years ago is having a marked effect on people's collecting habits. Space being at a premium, the emphasis today is on small items. In antique furniture, for example, small occasional tables, sewing tables and davenports are much in demand, whereas massive sideboards and four-poster beds are relatively unpopular simply because most people cannot house them. It is hardly surprising, therefore, that among the antiques of the future which are now exciting a great deal of interest are various 'miniatures'. In this category one may include items originally intended for use by children. Dolls' houses, dolls' furniture, dolls' costumes and dolls themselves are good examples of this, though these were not originally meant as playthings, but rather to give useful instruction in household management. Toy soldiers, too, always had a more serious purpose than mere playthings. From Frederick the Great to Winston Churchill, many future generals and strategists first learned the rudiments of warfare on the nursery floor, and today war-gaming is a serious pursuit, regarded by its many exponents as an exact science.

While toys do stretch back into the mists of prehistory, they did not become universally popular to any extent till the late nineteenth century. Early toys are rare because of the hard usage to which they were usually subjected, and because they were often thrown away when their owners grew up. The Victorian period, however, offers a vast field, and there are now many dealers in America and Europe who specialize in toys and dolls from about 1850 onwards.

The other category of miniature objects consists of reproductions of large-scale objects as models. Mankind has always been intrigued by the miniaturization of familiar things—bronze figurines and terracotta statuettes have survived since the classical age of Greece and Rome—but the advent of the Industrial Revolution in the eighteenth century gave the production of models a more serious application. It is interesting to reflect that the era which saw the wonderful ship models fashioned out of bone by French prisoners of war also witnessed the emergence of the utilitarian shipbuilder's model, designed to attract potential customers or to test new principles in naval architecture and marine engineering.

SCALE MODELS

Model-making is one of the oldest hobbies known to mankind. It is found in every society, no matter how primitive, and the motives for it are as varied as the models themselves. Models used in scientific or engineering experiments have a surprising antiquity. Hero of Alexandria, writing in AD 120, described a model constructed to demonstrate the kinetic properties of steam, thereby anticipating by many centuries the model engines constructed by Newcomen and Watt.

The first practical steam engine was that constructed by James Watt as part of the laboratory equipment of Glasgow University. In his later experiments he was assisted by William Murdoch, who, in 1786, built what was probably the first model locomotive in existence. This tiny locomotive had a cylinder barely $\frac{3}{4}$ inch in diameter.

Models, principally of ships, aircraft, locomotives and motor cars, are produced for several reasons. They are commonly used for the demonstration of inventions and for experiments by engineering firms and private inventors. They are employed as visual aids in schools and colleges, in technical training, in industry and the Armed Forces. A growing demand for models of all kinds comes from commercial organizations who require accurate working models for advertising and publicity. The advantage of miniaturized reproductions is that it becomes possible to demonstrate their capacity at exhibitions, often in a limited space.

Complete scale models are used for many purposes by transport companies, while sectional models are often produced in order to explain internal construction and the operation of specific parts. A more recent development is the use of models by architects, surveyors and town planners. Whether such models, which are generally large and cumbersome, will ever have the same appeal to posterity as the mobile type remains to be seen.

Model making simply as a hobby was for very many years almost exclusively British, but since the Second World War the craze for miniature locomotives, model aircraft and remote-controlled power boats has spread to Europe and America. The enthusiasm for scale models in Britain is like a pyramid. At the

151

broad base are countless thousands of devotees who subscribe to at least seven commercial periodicals on the subject, and support a growing industry, headed by the giant Lines Brothers combine (Triang–Hornby–Meccano) as well as several other firms producing die-cast metal and plastic models by the million. If Dinky cars and Hornby trains sound like 'kids' stuff' one's ideas are speedily revised when it is realized that pre-war Dinky cars are keenly sought after by adult collectors who will pay £10 ($24) or more for certain models. The scarcity of early Dinkies in mint condition may be accounted for by the excessively hard wear to which they were invariably subjected by their youthful owners.

Rather higher in the scale are the modellers who work from kits of components. There is little sign as yet that such items have a resale value, far less an 'antique' appreciation, though a notable exception is vintage Meccano. Early red and green outfits may fetch up to £300 ($720), depending on condition and completeness. Meccano models have now been elevated to the dignity of 'antiques'—an early kit made up as an Edwardian omnibus was spotted recently in an antique shop in England.

The élite of the modelling world, however, are the craftsmen who work in their own homes and construct beautifully detailed masterpieces of engineering, often from the simplest materials. These models form the centrepiece of the Model Engineer Exhibition, held annually in London's Seymour Hall.

Christie's introduced sales of models in October 1966 and held two that season, totalling over £40,000 ($96,000) each, the highlights of which were a 3½-inch gauge model of an American Rio Grande locomotive (1870) at 1300 guineas ($3276), and an American horse-drawn fire engine of the same period which went for 2800 guineas ($6860). Models vary in value, from £40–£50 ($96–$120) for wooden models of coaches to several hundred pounds for working models of steam locomotives.

'Off the peg' working models are available from time to time from shipping companies, airlines and transport firms. British Rail (Scottish Region) recently disposed of six model steam locomotives and five diesel-electric locomotives, plus a large quantity of model carriages and accessories, to collectors. Several firms specialize in buying, selling and exchanging scale models old and new, the best being Beattie's of London.

MODEL SOLDIERS

The earliest soldiers were made from pure tin, but gradually a greater amount of lead was added to produce a more durable alloy. These 'tin' soldiers were 'flats'—two-dimensional pieces in low relief mounted on small stands. The earliest soldiers also varied considerably in size, and it was not until 1848 that the famous manufacturer, Heinrichsen, adopted the 30-mm Nuremburg scale for his models.

To the French we probably owe the introduction of *rond bosse* or 'solid' figures about a century ago, and many of the famous manufacturers, particularly Heyde of Dresden, produced enormous quantities of them. Most of them were destined for export, since German collectors maintained a curiously conservative liking for flats—as, indeed, they do to this day.

The model soldier industry was revolutionized, however, seventy-five years ago when William Britain of London invented a process for hollow-cast, three-dimensional figures. Britain's soldiers were not only more realistic than their German counterparts, but, requiring far less metal, were considerably cheaper and rapidly captured the British market.

These soldiers were standardized to the No. 1 model railway gauge, and thus were on the large scale of 54 mm, still popular in that country. Today, Britain is the largest manufacturer of model soldiers in the world. Since 1966, however, lead alloy has been superseded by plastics, and it remains to be seen whether the latter will have the same appeal to the connoisseur.

Britain's lead soldiers originally sold for a few pence upwards, depending on whether the figure was mounted or on foot. In 1967, when they were still being marketed, they retailed at 2s 6d (30¢) (foot) to 4s (48¢) (mounted). One might be lucky enough to find a toy shop with a few boxes of Britain's lead soldiers at that price, but already relative scarcity has enhanced their value among collectors.

The early Britain models may be recognized by their round, instead of square, bases: the former are now highly prized and change hands at anything from 10s ($1.20) to 15s ($1.80) each, while such famous sets as the Royal Engineers balloon and winch-wagon or pontoon-bridge fetch as many pounds. Other firms whose lead soldiers are highly regarded for their accuracy and realistic postures were John Hill (Johillco) and Malleable Mouldings.

For those who are unable to produce distinctive items for themselves there are, at a price, the intricate collectors' pieces which have become increasingly popular in the past decade.

First in this field were the figures modelled by Charles Stadden. These figures, particularly those on the 54-mm scale, have a fantastic amount of detail in them. The portraiture alone is exceptionally lively, and the variety of postures of which these figures is capable is very wide.

In purchasing these models one has to pay for the labour and artistic skill which goes into their manufacture. Thus they vary in price from about £3 10s ($8) for a figure on foot, to 15 guineas ($37) for a mounted figure. Special pieces, such as standard-bearers and historic personages, may cost up to 20 guineas ($50).

Each figure is hand-modelled and painted, so that the result is a sculpture in miniature whose value will stand the test of time. Stadden also produces figures in 30 mm and 20 mm, the latter being particularly popular with war-gamers.

Russell Gamage (of 45 Sunborne Road, London SE7) manu-factures models under the name of Rose Miniatures and has also developed model-making into a fine art in the past ten years. His figures are noteworthy for their realism and the excellence of their finish. The prices for Gamage figures are comparable to the Stadden models. Both are also available unpainted so that the collector of more modest means but unlimited patience can do this work for himself.

Model soldiers, both mass produced and hand-made, are available from Norman Newton (44 Dover Street, W1) or The Collectors' Shop (Brady's Arcade, Kingston upon Thames). For hand-made figures by leading craftsmen—such as Stadden, Courtenay, Ping, Greenwood and Ball—Hummel, of Burlington Arcade, London W1, has the best general stock, though most dealers in arms, armour and war-medals are now turning in-creasingly to this facet of militaria.

DOLLS

Doll collecting has been developing since the 1920s, but it is only within the past decade that a meticulous, almost scientific, ap-proach has been adopted by collectors and students, and the tendency now, as in other forms of collecting, is to specialize in one aspect of dolls. One facet now attracting more attention is the wax doll, usually regarded as a peculiarly English invention.

Wax modelling had its origins in Italy, where an industry was born at the end of the Middle Ages for the production of religious figures in wax. These early wax figures had beautifully modelled heads, though their rag bodies were often rather crudely fashioned. Wax figures were used in funeral ceremonies in many parts of Europe. The fashion for wax portraits and cameos in the eighteenth century helped to develop the techniques employed so skilfully by the dollmakers of the following century.

154

Dolls as playthings are of comparatively recent date—certainly in Western Europe, where the transition from babyhood to adulthood was short and sharp. The need for toys was not widely recognized until the early nineteenth century, and it is only from this date that dolls are found in any quantity.

Early nineteenth-century dolls were either of wood or rag (for everyday play), or with porcelain heads (for Sunday use). A compromise was the wax doll, which came into popularity in the 1820s. The wax was poured into moulds to form a solid head and bust, the rest of the body being constructed of wood or fabric as before. Gradually wax was introduced for the hands and, at a later date, for the limbs as well.

A more imaginative treatment was devised in the 1840s, and consisted of anything up to a dozen layers of wax applied to a head moulded in metal or papier-mâché. Such dolls are known as ball-heads or slit-heads, the latter term derived from the practice of inserting the hair into the scalp by means of slits. A major disadvantage of the slit-head doll is the tendency for the slits to develop into long cracks spreading across the face and shoulders. Alternatively, the head and hair could be moulded in one piece; such 'squash-head' dolls are less attractive, but have generally survived in better condition than the slit-heads.

The wax doll industry was revolutionized in the 1850s by the Montanari family, Augusta and her son Richard Napoleon, who invented new techniques which resulted in wax dolls of great beauty and realism. The hair, eyelashes and eyebrows were painstakingly inserted into the wax one at a time with a hot needle.

At the Great Exhibition of 1851 Augusta Montanari was awarded a special prize for her exceedingly lifelike dolls. On account of the labour involved in their production, the Montanari dolls were very expensive, 5 guineas ($12.60) being charged for an undressed doll. Henry d'Allemagne, commenting on these dolls at the Paris Exposition of 1882, stated that their prices were prohibitive for general trade. As a result, relatively few of them have come down to posterity.

Wax dolls were also manufactured in England by the Pierotti family, which had been engaged in wax-modelling as long ago as 1780: as recently as 1930 Pierotti dolls could still be bought at Hamleys in Regent Street.

The only indigenous British wax doll-maker of note was Charles Marsh, who specialized in wax over papier-mâché. His blonde, blue-eyed dolls, produced in the latter years of the nineteenth century, had a distinctive 'English' appearance.

Wax dolls by these manufacturers are surprisingly cheap today, compared with their cost when new. Solid wax dolls vary from £20 ($48) upwards; those with an identifiable mark by Montanari, Pierotti or Marsh may be worth from £50 ($120) upwards. Portrait dolls are highly prized, and fetch correspondingly high prices.

The rising interest in dolls is demonstrated by the growth of literature on the subject. *Dolls and Dollmakers* by Mary Hillier (Weidenfeld and Nicholson) ranges in time from Egyptian dolls of 2000 BC to the latest 'Play Safe' dolls, and covers the world from England to Japan and from Baffin Land to the Falklands. As its title implies, a considerable portion of the book is devoted to the craftsmen who evolved the doll from the primitive pegwooden to the talking doll of today. Mrs Hillier combines a wealth of scholarship with entertainment in a book that is as readable as it is informative.

9 Motor cars

Barely eighty years have elapsed since Gottlieb Daimler mounted a small internal combustion engine on a tricycle and gave the world its first petrol-driven motor car. Although this invention is of comparative youth, there are few people alive today who can look back to a time when the roads were free of cars. Nowadays, in North America, Britain and the countries of Western Europe, the ratio of private cars to the population is increasing daily. The car is no longer a luxury and a joy to possess, but a necessity which it is a chore to drive. The children of today, who fret and whine, trapped and strapped in the back of the car while their father (or, more often than not these days, their mother) struggles to negotiate the snarl-ups and road jams, will become, in turn, a generation of motorists regarding the car as a necessary evil.

Mass produced by the multi-million, its 'built-in obsolescence' all too apparent, the modern motor car in most cases cannot be regarded an an object of beauty or enduring qualities. In a sense the public merely get what they ask for: a machine which will get them from A to B with no nonsense about it. A few cars, however, continue the age-old traditions of the coach-builder's art and are worth buying today as antiques of the future. The greater element of craftsmanship, of precision engineering and handwork involved in the production of an Aston-Martin DB6 is certainly reflected in its current retail price, but is it expensive? Expensiveness is not a factor which is relevant when considering a car of this quality. Long after its contemporaries off the mass production assembly line have been consigned to the scrap yard, these Aston-Martins will still be giving good service and, if looked after properly, their value will have been enhanced rather than diminished.

Since Daimler put his first spluttering horseless carriage on the road it is estimated that there have been about five thousand makes of car throughout the world. Of these probably fewer than one per cent are really in the category of timeless classics. Such,

157

however, is the demand nowadays for fine examples of the cars of yesteryear that the sights have been lowered, and virtually any car more than fifty years old is eagerly snapped up simply on account of its age. This demand undoubtedly stems from a nostalgia for the good old prewar days when pleasure motoring had some real meaning; petrol was little more than a shilling (12¢) a gallon and there were few hindrances, in the form of traffic lights, zebra crossings, box junctions—and other motor cars—to impede one's enjoyment of the open road. A generation of motorists has grown up, however, who have no intimate recollection of prewar driving, and yet the interest in old cars is increasing rapidly. Some other reason must exist to explain this interest. I believe that this is a reaction against modern, streamlined mass production techniques in the motor industry. It may also be a form of inverted snobbery; instead of competing on the same terms with the neighbour's sleek modern car, it is a sort of 'one-upmanship' to sport a vintage.

Just as antiques are defined by age, so old cars are classified, in Britain, by when they were manufactured. Veterans are cars manufactured in the pioneer years up to 1904; Edwardians date from 1905 to the end of the First World War (1919); Vintage cars are those which were produced in the decade of the Roaring Twenties. Age is the sole criterion for inclusion in the Veteran and Edwardian classes, but, in theory at least, one ought to qualify the Vintage criterion by adding that the term strictly applies to sports cars of the period 1920–30, since the term 'Vintage' was first coined by the Vintage Sports Car Club. A fourth category, the Post-Vintage Thoroughbreds (or PVTS), caters for post-1930 cars whose design and overall quality is in the classic Vintage tradition. All four categories are worth investing in; indeed, the growth rate of this particular form of collecting has outpaced most of the others in the past decade. Each class of collectable car is examined in some detail below.

VETERANS AND EDWARDIANS

The British have always shown a peculiar interest in the horseless carriage—which seems strange in view of the strong interest in horses which runs parallel to it! From the time of Trevithick, at the beginning of the nineteenth century, Englishmen were greatly preoccupied with the development of self-propelled vehicles. Successive Acts of Parliament, from 1832 onwards, however, saw to it that this development was literally kept on the right rails. While Britain developed the most complex railway network of any country in the world, the roads were kept free of horseless carriages by restrictive legislation. Britain takes the credit for the steam engine and the steam locomotive, but it was left to the Germans, Americans and French to produce the earliest internal combustion engines and 'automobiles'. As late as 1896, a decade after the first Daimler and Benz cars appeared, British motorists were hampered by the notorious Red Flag Act, which required motor cars to be preceded by a man waving a red flag as a warning to pedestrians and other (horse-drawn) traffic. The passing of the Locomotives and Highways Act 1896, permitting vehicles to run at twelve miles an hour without a man preceding them, was celebrated by the Emancipation run from London to Brighton, since commemorated annually by the Veteran Car Club.

Despite prolonged official antipathy to the car in Britain, it is ironic to note that it is in that country that an affection for old cars has always been strongest. The Veteran Car Club, founded at Brighton in November 1930, is the oldest of its kind in the world—five years older than the comparable Antique Automobile Club of the United States and the Association des Propriétaires de Vieilles Voitures Automobiles ('Les Teuf-Teuf') of France. The vcc was formed by a group of enthusiasts who were anxious that the earliest cars should be preserved while a few of them still existed. Membership grew very slowly in the prewar years, and more or less stood still in the early part of the Second World War. In September 1945, when the Club's first postwar rally was held, its membership stood at a mere 300, owning about 180 cars—and these figures were, in fact, a great improvement on the prewar numbers, largely because of the decision, taken in 1943, to throw membership open to the owners of Edwardians (then regarded as vehicles manufactured between 1904 and 1916). In the immediate postwar years membership progressed rapidly, so that by the time of the Club's Silver Jubilee rally in 1955 there were 1300 members owning over a thousand cars.

The highlight of the Club's activities is the annual and much-publicized London to Brighton Commemoration Run. The highly successful comedy film *Genevieve*, based on the 1952 run, did more than anything else to stimulate interest in Veteran cars; in every country where it was screened flagging enthusiasm for old cars revived and interest was born where it had never existed before. From Britain to New Zealand the impact of this film was tremendous. Many old cars, whose existence was unknown or long forgotten, were brought to light as a result of the publicity this remarkable film gave to the hobby. In the United States the film inspired a number of 'Genevieve' rallies, including a creditable imitation of the London to Brighton Run by the Horseless Carriage

Club of Colorado (from Denver to Brighton, Colo.). The screening of *Genevieve* in the mid-1950s was undoubtedly the turning-point in the interest shown in Veteran cars, and the movement which aims at their preservation has gone from strength to strength ever since.

Naturally, the number of Veterans available has failed to keep pace with the growing interest and demand. The number of new finds has significantly decreased in recent years, and the time must rapidly approach when the last of the pre-1905 cars in the world has been unearthed and lovingly restored to as near its pristine condition as possible. Strange tales have been told of old cars found in the oddest places: of the 1902 M.M.C. found in a cellar completely covered in books, of one old-timer which performed sterling service for many years as a hen-house, of others found in almost immaculate condition in farmyard buildings and hay-barns. When the vcc was in its infancy its members would scour the scrap yards and secondhand dealers' establishments and pick up rare vehicles for a few pounds at most. Often enough these vehicles would be in the last stages of disintegration, and a considerable amount of time, money, energy and expertise would be required to restore them to their original appearance. Thus the market in Veteran cars has always been a hard one. Few Veteran owners would willingly part with their cars, and it is true to say that to the *aficionado* these vehicles are beyond price. At one time the only way to acquire a Veteran car was to go out and track one down—never an easy task, this is now virtually impossible.

Although the value of Veterans has soared enormously in recent years, at least it is slightly easier—given a limitless cheque book—to purchase a Veteran car which has already been restored and lovingly maintained. Motor vehicles have entered the hallowed realms of the top auctioneers, in Britain, France, the United States and elsewhere. In 1969, for example, Sotheby's held two important sales of Veteran, Edwardian, Vintage and Post-Vintage Thoroughbred cars, and several hundred vehicles came under the hammer. Regular sales of old cars have also been held in recent years by Ader and Picard of Paris. Sotheby's New York associates, Parke-Bernet, have also conducted a number of important car sales. Among the top prices paid in the past few years for Veteran and Edwardian cars are $45,000 (£18,750) for a 1913 Mercer raceabout, and £5,200 ($12,480) for a 1904 Gladiator.

Just as *Genevieve* stimulated interest in Veterans in the 1950s, so the musical *Chitty-Chitty-Bang-Bang* has helped to maintain interest at a high level. The 'star' of this film is the giant 1907 Napier 60

160

horsepower sports two-seater. Its incredible engine capacity is almost eight litres and the 45-gallon tank gives the car a cruising range of 300 miles. When new it retailed in Britain at £945 ($2268). In the Sotheby's sale in October 1968 it made £7500 ($18,000).

Veteran cars, strictly speaking, are those manufactured before the end of 1904, in which year the speed limit was raised from 12 to 20 m.p.h. This date is also significant, since it marks the dividing line between the pioneers and prototypes (some of which are most weird in appearance) and the period when design had become concentrated on the basic type of vehicle which constitutes the modern motor car. Edwardian cars are regarded as those dating from 1905 to the end of the First World War. This classification seems to have been first suggested by Francis Hutton-Stott in January 1938, but five years elapsed before the term was adopted and Edwardianism officially brought under the wing of the vcc. In a sense the Edwardian car seemed to fall between two stools; neither had it attracted, at that time, the antiquarian interest of the Veterans, nor had it progressed to the technical perfection which was the hallmark of the Vintage car. Nevertheless, these giants—the 8-litre Napier referred to above was of modest proportions compared with the 10-litre 90 h.p. Fiat of 1910, the 12-litre G.P. Itala of 1908 or the stupendous 15-litre G.P. Lorraine Dietrich of 1912—could often hold their own with the sports cars of the twenties, and it was inevitable that they should hold the interest of the Vintage Sports Car enthusiasts and eventually formed a valuable link between the Veterans and Vintage cars. By the time of the outbreak of the Second World War the Edwardians had come of age and begun to assume an air of relative antiquity. Wartime salvage drives, however, threatened to remove for ever from the scene many of these fine old cars, which appeared to have outlived their usefulness; so the active interest of the Veteran Car Club in saving them for posterity was timely.

VINTAGE CARS

In November 1934 a small group of motoring enthusiasts gathered in London to form a club catering for their interest in the fine, hand-made cars of the previous decade. They were linked by a common dislike of modern production techniques in the motor industry, the poor qualities and indifferent design of the modern car—all factors which were accelerated by the industrial depression of 1929–30. These enthusiasts called themselves the Vintage Sports Car Club, and membership was limited to those owning cars produced before the end of 1930. An interesting point emerges

L

from this; barely four years had elapsed from the date set as the criterion of interest. It is idle to speculate what might have happened in the world of antiques today had a similar band of enthusiasts got together a century earlier and begun consciously to preserve the best of the Regency and previous eras so soon after their end. The formation of the vscc in 1934 also emphasizes the fact that an object need not be old to be desirable and worth preserving. By the time that objects have attained great antiquity so few examples have been preserved that it is often their scarcity, rather than age or any other criterion, which makes them worth collecting.

Although the arbitrary date of 1930 has been retained by the vscc, necessitated by the rules and regulations of the club governing competitive motoring events, the Club has retained some flexibility by recognizing that fine car production did not come to an abrupt halt in that year, and since the Second World War membership has been extended to owners of post-1930 cars of the 'thoroughbred' class. The Club has grown from the original handful of members to almost 4000, and is still going from strength to strength, testifying to the growing interest in fine-quality cars of this type. The use of the adjective 'Vintage' in the context of motor cars is particularly apt. Just as the factors which combine to produce a vintage wine are numerous, so also the points which put a car in the true vintage class are many and diverse. The development of the manufacturing company over many years, the experience and expertise of designers, engineers, coach-builders and craftsmen, the skill and care lavished on the manufacture, the combination of the right engine with the right chassis—these are the major factors which affect every car, and to their presence, or absence, is due the right of any car to the title of vintage. While these general factors can be more or less constant for all the cars produced by certain top-quality manufacturers, such as Rolls-Royce, it often happens that one particular model, over a period of years, is so outstanding as to eclipse the remainder, good though they may be. Thus while any Rolls-Royce of the vintage period is highly desirable, the most sought after models today are the Phantoms; and of these the Phantom II, produced between 1929 and 1936, is regarded as the finest. Moreover, in that seven-year period Rolls Royce produced no fewer than sixteen distinct series of this model, all containing subtle refinements on earlier series. These series were designated by groups of two or three letters, and of these possibly the PY chassis, short Continental Touring Phantom was as near to the perfect car as the motorist could ever get.

The Continental Phantom was first produced in 1932—two

years outside the date-line set by the VSCC—and this only goes to show how impracticable a date criterion can be in judging the quality of anything, whether it be cars, porcelain or glassware. The great Hispano-Suiza and Isotta-Fraschini sports cars of the 1930s are also outside the vintage period, as are the Bentleys and Aston-Martins of the present day, but they are collectable none the less.

Yet, as far as vintage cars are concerned, the main criterion to the collector these days, is the date. The VSCC set the trend of applying this term primarily to sports models, and this is understandable, since the best cars in the twenties and thirties were produced for the more exacting requirements of the sports motorist. Nevertheless, such is the demand by collectors nowadays that even the humble Austin Seven and its American counterpart, the Ford Model-T, have acquired a cachet of respectability and been raised to the status of collectors' pieces. It is interesting to note that no fewer than fifteen million of the latter were produced between 1908 and 1927; yet a 'Tin Lizzie' of 1914, in good condition, made £2000 ($4800) at a Sotheby auction in June 1968.

There are, in fact, fewer than a score of makes of car which can truly be considered as vintage in every sense of the word. These are the 'blue chips' of the era between the wars, and they are the cars in greatest demand, attracting the keenest bidding at auction. Lest I be accused of partiality to any one make, I have listed them below in alphabetical order.

ALFA-ROMEO

Alfa (Anonima Lombarda Fabbrica Automobili), founded in 1910, combined with the engineer and car designer, Nicola Romeo, just before the First World War to form the famous Alfa-Romeo company. Very few of the early postwar Alfa Romeos are now in existence, the beautiful RLSS or 22/90, but the 1·5-litre Turismo, which appeared in 1927 and was very popular on the Continent, is rather more plentiful. A variant of this was the Gran Turismo, enlarged in 1929 and given a 1750-cc engine, which dominated the Irish TT in that year and 1930. The following year Alfa-Romeo developed the giant 2·3-litre 8-cylinder car whose engine ranks as one of the finest pieces of precision engineering to be found under any bonnet. Meticulous attention to detail and finish was the hallmark of these Alfa-Romeos, whose engineers and designers were said to have the blood of Cellini and Michelangelo coursing through their veins! It is certainly true to say that

163

few cars have ever evoked such praise, and often in the least expected quarter. This car even drew Henry Ford's unqualified admiration; 'When I see an 8-cylinder Alfa Romeo,' he said on one occasion, 'I take off my hat!' In 1934 Alfa-Romeo produced a 2·9-litre version to meet the rising challenge of Mercédès-Benz. Very few of these magnificent cars were put on the market on account of their exorbitant cost, and today it ranks as one of the major rarities among Post-Vintage Thoroughbreds.

ASTON-MARTIN

This famous make of sports car takes its name from Lionel Martin, who designed and built the cars, and the Buckinghamshire village of Aston Clinton, whose hill-climb course was a favourite testing-ground for sports cars before the Second World War. Martin's first car was a combination of an Isotta-Fraschini chassis and a Coventry Simplex 1·5-litre engine which he built for his own use. In the 1920s the Aston-Martin company built a small quantity of 1·5-litre 'side valve', and these are the most eagerly sought after cars of this *marque* today. In 1927 the standard 1·5-litre came on the market (retailing at £625, $1500), and was popular with sports motorists in the ensuing decade. A change in the company's policy resulted, in 1936, in the short-lived and not very popular 2-litre, which, in turn, was superseded shortly before the outbreak of war by the 2-litre Atom—a very scarce model, since the Second World War intervened before it could be produced on a commercial basis. After the war the company changed hands, but the traditions of superb craftsmanship have been faithfully maintained, and the postwar Aston-Martins, produced since 1948, rank among the modern 'classics'.

BALLOT

Few people today, outside Vintage Sports Car circles, will have heard of this make of car, named after its designer Ernest Ballot. These lovely cars, whether it be the 2-litre 4-cylinder model of 1923–8, or the RH3 'straight eight' of 1929–30, are among the *rarae aves* of the motoring world. It has been reckoned that fewer than a dozen exist in Britain, and probably no more in their country of origin, France. Of these the rarest is undoubtedly the first of the *marque* which appeared in 1922. Very few of them were produced, though they remained current till 1925. The first of the 2-litres was followed in 1923 by the Touring version which is the one most commonly seen today (if one can use such an adverb when discussing the Ballot). This in turn was superseded by the Touring Sports version of 1925, and two years later the 8-cylinder RH made its debut. In appearance the RH3 was a most attractive car with a long, low bonnet and beautiful coupé coachwork. The promise of the first decade was not fulfilled, however, since the Ballot company was absorbed by Hispano-Suiza in 1929, and production of these lovely vehicles ceased abruptly. They very seldom come on the market, and now must be regarded as true collectors' pieces.

BENTLEY

The name Bentley is a household word to this day for luxury cars of the highest—and most expensive—order, but the sleek tycoon's limousine of today is a far cry from the magnificent sports cars of the twenties, which even now can show a clean pair of heels in motor trials and rallies. W.O. Bentley entered the motor-car business as long ago as 1910, and even before the First World War was making a name for himself in racing circles with his adaptation of the French D.F.P. tourer, in which he established a prewar record for the Aston Clinton hill climb. His experience in designing aero engines during the war stood him in good stead when, in 1919, he began to evolve the perfect fast touring car. The prototype was exhibited at the Motor Show that year, but almost two years elapsed before the first of the famous 3-litre Bentleys were available to a discriminating public. In the twenties Bentley produced such renowned cars as the Big Six, the 4½-litre and the Speed Six, which scooped the pool in most of the racing events of that decade. At Le Mans from 1927 to 1930 Bentleys won every year; in 1929 Bentleys actually took the first four places! Bentleys were never cheap cars (varying from £1200 ($2880) for the 3-litre to £2400 ($5760) for the Speed Six), but because Bentley believed that a first-class job was of paramount importance, the company's profit margin was usually very slender. It is not surprising that the manufacturers of prestige cars should have suffered so badly as a result of the Depression of 1930 and, inevitably, the original Bentley Company went out of production the following year. Bentley's 'swan song' was the stupendous 8-litre, the sensation of the motoring world in 1931. Fewer than a hundred were produced before the company went out of business, but all of them are in the loving hands of connoisseurs today.

The assets of Bentley Motors were acquired by Rolls-Royce in 1932, and since that date the name has come to mean all that is sumptuous and luxurious in elegant motoring. In general, it would be true to say that any Bentley of the post-1931 era, like its sports

165

predecessors, would be a good investment, provided that it has been reasonably maintained and its coachwork is sound. From the collector's viewpoint, however, the best of the postwar Bentleys is reckoned to be the R Type Continental.

BUGATTI

It has been said, with a great deal of justification, that Ettore Bugatti designed cars 'in much the same way as a court clock-maker of the eighteenth century would design and build a time-piece for his royal patron'. His brother, Rembrandt Bugatti, was an artist and sculptor of note, and something of the artist was certainly in the blood of 'Le Patron', as the car designer was known. The Bugattis were perfectionists in everything—in the horses they bred, in the fine liqueurs distilled from their own vineyards, in their connoisseurship of good food. Their father, Carlo Bugatti, was an all-rounder—artist, sculptor and metalworker in the best traditions of Cellini; Ettore was more of a Michelangelo. Had he lived during the Italian Renaissance he would have made his mark as a designer of splendid churches, as a sculptor or painter. Born four centuries later, however, he established an international reputation as a designer of the most blue-blooded of all vintage cars. It is significant that Bugatti's early training was artistic, but his main love was motoring. His first car—a twin-engined tri-cycle—was built when he was only eighteen. The following year (1900) he built a 4-cylinder car which was an immediate success. In 1910 he set up as a car manufacturer on his own, and the first fruits of this venture were the petite 4-cylinder sports cars of 1911 onwards. His factory, at Molsheim in Alsace, had to suspend activities during the First World War, but by 1920 the first of the Type 13 Bugattis were in production. Bugatti was a prolific designer—more than seventy models were evolved in the two decades up to 1939 when the Nazi invasion of Alsace put an end to car production at Molsheim for good.

Of the many types of Bugatti the Type 57, produced during the last five years of the company, is probably the best known and likeliest to be found on the roads today. The most expensive and sumptuous of all the Bugattis, however, was the aptly named Royale, manufactured from 1927 onwards. Only seven were built—primarily for Bugatti himself and a very few favoured customers, who included King Carol of Roumania and King Alfonso of Spain, and the chassis alone retailed at just under £6000 ($14,400); the most expensive Rolls of that period was sold for less than a third of that sum. The engine capacity was

166

almost 15 litres—a staggering figure—and it was capable of 125 m.p.h. with ease. Only once in each generation is a Royale likely to come on the market, and it would be futile to assess the value of the half dozen now in existence, but even the humbler Types 35, 37 and 57 fetch extremely high prices well in excess of their initial cost, proving once again that the very best makes the best investment.

DUESENBERG

It is a curious fact that in the United States, the most 'motorized' country in the world, there has seldom been produced a really top-quality car. Among the few exceptions were the cars designed and built by the German brothers Frederick and August Duesenberg between 1920 and 1937. Of these the best were the luxurious J and SJ models of the 1930s; the chassis cost well over £2000 ($4800), and on it coachwork of comparable magnificence was built. Fewer than 500 of these lovely cars were produced—a ridiculously small number considering the size of the American market—and very few of them were ever exported to Europe. It is interesting to note that an attempt to recapture the magic and prestige associated with the name of Duesenberg resulted in the four-door sedan produced in 1966. This prototype, which was never put into production, fetched $37,500 at a Parke-Bernet sale of Post-Vintage Thoroughbred cars in May 1968.

DELAGE

Louis Delage began producing cars as long ago as 1906 but, like many of the other great names in Vintage Sports-Cars, it was not until after the First World War that the company achieved international distinction. The 14/40 2-litre Type DI made its debut at the end of 1924 and was very popular with the smart set in Britain in the late twenties. It was followed in 1926 by the Sport, the Special Sport and the Grand Sport, by which Delage progressed to bigger and more powerful models. The *chef d'œuvre* was the 'straight-eight', the D8.5S100, which is regarded as one of the finest tourers of the vintage period. The Delage company was taken over by Delahaye in 1935, and the principal outcome of this was the D8.120, which appeared in 1937. Since the Second World War attempts have been made to relaunch the Delage, but without much success so far.

This outstanding sports car was current for some fifteen years (1924–39) and underwent numerous modifications during that period. Basically it had a 1·5-litre 6-cylinder engine, but the large range of standard types could be further varied by amendments to suit the requirements of the individual motorist. This car evolved steadily over the years, and it is reckoned that the models built from 1930 onwards are more desirable today. Among the popular models which are eagerly sought by vintage connoisseurs these days are the Anzani, Boulogne, T.T. Replica, Shelsley and Nurburg types.

HISPANO–SUIZA

At the end of the nineteenth century the unlikely combination of a Swiss engineer, Marc Birkigt, and a group of Barcelona financiers resulted in the foundation of the Société de Construction d'Automobiles, whose cars were named Hispano-Suiza in honour of the union. After the First World War the company established factories at Bois Colombes near Paris. Like many of his contemporaries, Birkigt spent the war years manufacturing aero engines, and this experience was drawn on in the 1920s in the production of cars such as the 6·5-litre Hispano-Suiza. This superb car was extremely expensive (the chassis cost £2200 ($5280) in 1920, a world record at the time), and some highly distinctive coachwork was built on to it in luxurious styles befitting such a princely car. The car had a remarkably long life in current production, being manufactured as late as 1933. An 8-litre version appeared in 1922 and remained in current production during the same period. It was superseded in 1931–2 by a 5-litre 6-cylinder car known as the Type-68. Its larger brother, the 68-bis, was a fantastic vehicle with an engine capacity of 11,310 cc and a petrol consumption of 10 miles to the gallon. In its heyday it almost rivalled the J-type Duesenberg in cost and, Bugatti's Royale apart, was the most magnificent creation on four wheels.

ISOTTA–FRASCHINI

At the turn of the century Cesare Isotta and Oreste Fraschini formed a company for the manufacture of motor cars in Milan, but it was not until after the First World War that Isotta-Fraschini burst on the international scene with the Type-8, a luxury car in the same class as the great Hispano-Suizas. Variations of this were the Super Spinto of 1926 and the 8-B of 1931. The latter represented the ultimate in the Isotta *marque* and remained in production till the outbreak of war. It is the version most highly sought after nowadays. After the Second World War an attempt was made to revive the fortunes of the company, and a new version, the 8C or Monterosa, was displayed at the Paris Salon of 1947; but apart from this prototype no Isotta-Fraschinis have gone into production for thirty years.

LAGONDA

'Some talk of a Lagonda', as the song puts it, but few who do are aware of the fact that this famous breed of sports car derived its name from the otherwise obscure town of Lagonda in Ohio, birthplace of Wilbur Gunn, who emigrated to England at the end of the nineteenth century and gradually built up a business as a mechanical engineer. From sewing machines and bicycles he progressed to motor vehicles, his earliest venture in this field being a rather curious tri-car with the driver and passenger mounted tandem-fashion. It was not, in fact, until some time after Gunn's death in 1920 that the familiar lines of the Lagonda sports cars began to appear. The first essay in this direction was a 2-litre car, produced in 1925, and this was followed by the 1100-cc Rapier, which remained in intermittent production until the Second World War.

It was the 4½-litre cars—the M45 Rapide, the L.G.45 and the L.G.6—produced between 1933 and 1939, however, which really put Lagondas on the map. In 1935 W.O.Bentley severed his connection with Rolls-Royce and went to work for Lagonda. His genius is evident in the Lagonda produced after that time, the L.G. types being his first projects. Stylistically the Bentley 4·5-litre Lagondas may be recognized by the mounting of the spare wheel and the tool box in wheel form, symmetrically on the offside and nearside wings respectively. Bentley's chief contribution to the elevation of the Lagonda company to the first rank of car manufacturers was the great V12, which made its debut in 1937. This noiseless giant could attain 100 m.p.h. with effortless ease—though the petrol consumption (12 miles to the gallon when new) and an equally wicked thirst for oil are points to be reckoned with in running a V12 today. Although V12s were in production for barely two years, they are reasonably plentiful today. Bearing in mind their heavy fuel consumption, they could have had little usage once war broke out; severe petrol rationing in Britain meant that most of these cars had to be laid up 'for the duration', and it was well into the 1950s before any of them would really have begun to show any signs of wear and tear. A V12 Lagonda in reasonable condition would be worth about £2000 ($4800) today—roughly double its list price when new—and it is a car which is only now beginning to attract antiquarian interest and a correspondingly enhanced value.

MERCÉDÈS–BENZ

Today the 'Merc' is the Continental equivalent of the Rolls-Royce —the household word for the best in luxury motoring. In the decade before the Second World War, however, it meant fast touring cars, the equal of Hispano-Suiza and the Bentley. The name itself was of an earlier period, having been bestowed by Karl Benz on a car of 1900 built in honour of Mercédès Jellinek. Benz amalgamated with Daimler in 1926, and thus it came about that Daimler's chief designer, a certain Dr Ferdinand Porsche, was responsible for producing the famous S-type Mercédès-Benz sports cars of 1927–39. They were highly popular when current, and large numbers of them were sold all over the world. Today, in its various forms, the S-type Mercédès is one of the most keenly sought after vintage cars. In the brief period between its debut in international competitive motoring in 1929 and the advent of the Nazi regime, the Mercédès-Benz S-types took almost a hundred 1st, 2nd or 3rd places in international races and hill climbs—no mean achievement. The Nazis slapped a heavy purchase tax on the Mercédès, so that most of the SS and SSK models of later years were sold abroad. According to J.R. Buckley, in *Cars for the Connoisseur*, only two examples of the 38/250 Mercédès exist in Germany, and both are in museums. The 540K Mercédès, first produced in 1936, is a comparatively rare car, since virtually every model was earmarked for the use of high-ranking *Parteigenosse*. Incidentally, in his sixties Dr Porsche became a freelance designer and, as such, was responsible for such world-famous vehicles as the Volkswagen and the Tiger tank— not to mention the Post-Vintage Thoroughbred sports cars of the present which still bear his name.

PACKARD

This name, a household word in the United States, means many different things to many different people, from trucks to family runabouts, mass produced for the American market. In the vintage field, however, the Packard company were responsible for one or

170

two models which are worthy of consideration as antiques of the future. Unfortunately these fine cars, the Packard 8-cylinder Speedster and the V12, went into production at a time when the Wall Street crash and the subsequent Depression of the 1930s hit the wealthy classes very badly. Thus relatively few of these fine cars were sold, and today they are regarded in America as real collectors' pieces.

ROLLS-ROYCE

Last, but by no means least, of the *marques* discussed in this chapter is the premier name in motoring—a position which has seldom been assailed in the past sixty years. Conscious of their standing in the motoring world, Rolls-Royce company has clung steadfastly to the classic lines of the radiator; like the pediment and pillars of a Greek temple, the Rolls radiator has a timeless quality, as suitable on the Silver Ghost of 1910 as it is on the latest Silver Shadow models. The sole change was the colour of the RR monogram, which was altered from red to black following Sir Henry Royce's death in 1933. To this timeless quality may be added the immutably high standards of Rolls-Royce cars. Of no other company can it be said that they have never produced a bad model, and today any Rolls-Royce may be regarded as a collector's item. It is too soon yet to judge the investment potential of postwar Rolls-Royces; they should still be available in reasonable condition at less than the original retail price, since they have not yet begun to attract antiquarian interest.

The vintage Rolls cars, however, are eminently collectable, and have been so for many years now; the market for them is fairly well established—though not stabilized, since prices continue to soar alarmingly. It has been estimated that the value of a good prewar Rolls has doubled in the past five years, and there is no sign of interest slackening, nor is there likely to be, in view of the enormous demand for them. The classic is the Silver Ghost, of which over 6000 were produced between 1907 and 1925. Not so long ago the top price for a superbly restored Ghost was £9800; then a staggering £9200 ($22,000) was paid for one in poor condition, although since then the same amount has been paid for a fine example in the sale of vintage vehicles held by Sotheby's in 1968. The Ghost was succeeded by the remarkable Phantom series. The Phantom I, which was in many respects a transitional car, sold moderately well (over 2000 in the four years it was current), but has not proved to be so popular with vintage enthusiasts as some of the other models in this *marque*. Consequently, good examples can still be picked up for £1800—£2500 ($4320–$6000), depending on condition. Under the brilliant supervision of W.O. Bentley, however, the Phantom II, which was manufactured from 1929 till 1935, turned out to be a much better car, and one which is eagerly sought after today. Bearing in mind the world economic situation at the time of its currency, it is not surprising that only 1767 Phantom IIs were made. Consequently, it is comparatively scarce today and prized (and priced) accordingly. The Phantom III, which appeared in 1936 and whose career was abruptly curtailed by the outbreak of the Second World War, is probably the best bet of all. For obvious reasons the best investment would be as late a model as possible, preferably one which was barely run in before petrol rationing put it off the road. For preference, therefore, the chassis numbers should be in the Sl or SH series.

With a quality car such as the Phantom, the customer was given a considerable amount of latitude in his choice of coachwork and body styling. Few could have been as bizarre as that of the Indian prince's Rolls which had a superstructure in the form of a swan, but the range of styles found on Phantoms is quite amazing. Generally speaking, unusual features in the coachwork are worth a premium. In the standard types the descending order of desirability is drophead coupé, saloon and 'hearse' styling (by the last-named I mean the Early English Perpendicular brand of stateliness which distinguished the Phantom Is).

Rolls-Royce also produced a range of relatively small, low-powered cars, the so-called 'ladies' Rolls', which appeared between 1922 and 1936 in various guises, until superseded by the Silver Wraith shortly before the war. These cars tend to be spurned by the true vintage enthusiast, and consequently are still comparatively cheap. Here again, the best models to go for are the Wraith and the later series of 20/25 which would have had low mileages before the war.

Unlike most of the other antiques of the future discussed in this book, motor cars were never meant to sit still and be purely decorative. Some degree of wear and tear is inevitable in even the best cared-for models. While it is true to say that the handful of makes which I have selected for discussion were renowned for their high standards of workmanship, incredible durability and built-in longevity, one must also bear in mind that much depends on the carefulness of the previous owners. The fewer owners the better is a maxim which applies only too well to old cars. What may seem a bargain at £1000 ($2400) may turn out to be a white elephant if £5000 ($12,000) is required to restore it. A similar car

172

at £2000, but requiring much less restoration, would naturally be a better investment. With old cars, as with any other form of collectable items, it pays to buy the best that one can afford at the very outset.

This chapter has been concerned mainly with the top names in vintage motoring, and space has precluded the mention of such worthwhile makes as Alvis, Lanchester, Rover, Talbot and many others. Moreover, the emphasis has been laid on the connoisseur class of vintage cars and ignored the great number of more humble vehicles which, in their own modest way, are still worthy of the collector's consideration. It is interesting to note that among the cars sold by Sotheby's on 24 October 1968 was an Austin Seven of 1926 which made £320 ($768) a useful premium over the £145 ($348) it cost when new, particularly bearing in mind the amount of use it had had in the ensuing forty odd years. Not only have collectors been lowering their sights so that any old car, whether one of the better *marques* or not, has become desirable but they are now extending their interest to include fairly recent models which do not really qualify for the epithet Post-Vintage Thoroughbred.

It is difficult to know exactly when an old car ceases to have the derogatory epithets 'second-hand' or 'used' and earns the title of a collector's piece. A perusal of the advertisements in the British motoring magazines reveals any amount of common-or-garden 'used' cars priced from £30 to £100 ($72–$240), but here and there emerges a Sunbeam Talbot 90 or a Riley Pathfinder priced at £250–£300 ($600–$720). Already the MG TCs of fifteen or twenty years ago are worth more than their original list price, and Jaguar sports cars, such as the XK120 or the XK140, are always in great demand. In the same way the E-type, with its aerodynamic styling, is obviously a car which should hold its value if looked after properly. Good, solid models which have been tipped as sound investments for the future include the Rover P4 range, the 60, 75, 80, 90, 95, 100, 105R, 105S and 110 models. Some 43,000 of the Rover 75 were produced, and the 90 ran to an edition of 36,000 altogether, so they are plentiful in reasonable condition at around the £250 ($600) mark. The British Automobile Association's magazine *Drive* in 1968 attempted to prophesy the cars of today which would be worth owning twenty years' hence, and came to the conclusion that the Austin Healey Sprite Mark I, the Standard Vanguard Phase I, the Triumph Mayflower, Sunbeam Talbot 90, Jaguar XK150 and Morris Minor Traveller came into this category. Some of the cars in this list are obvious, others are rather surprising, and it can only be conjectured to what extent this prophesy will be justified.

10 Commemorative and association items

The previous chapters have dealt with collectable objects, either according to the material which composes them or, in the case of Victoriana, according to a fairly well-defined period in which they were produced. There is a third method of grouping objects, however, and that is by virtue of the event or person which they serve to commemorate. The objects can either be commemorative in the strict sense, being produced specifically to perpetuate the memory of a person or an occasion, or they can be objects associated in some way with a person or event, and for that reason—and that reason alone—of interest to collectors. Both classes of object are collectable to a greater or lesser degree, depending on the importance of the person or thing commemorated and—in the latter case at any rate—depending on their provenance.

COMMEMORATIVE ITEMS

When talking of 'commemoratives' one tends to think of coins, medals and postage stamps, all objects to which the commemorative treatment has been applied with greater frequency in recent years. The commemorative idea has, however, been applied to other fields, and there are signs that this type of collecting is on the increase. It is difficult to determine when objects (other than medals and statuary) were first made for a commemorative purpose. Such objects were fashioned by the Greeks and the Romans, by the Persians, the Chinese and the Indians. In Western European terms commemorative pottery and silverware begins to be relatively plentiful from the seventeenth century onwards. Majolica and delft ware, commemorating the accession of King William of Orange is known, and several hundreds of pounds have been paid for fine examples of dishes bearing commemorative inscriptions and portraits of William and Mary.

174

The eighteenth century is replete with examples of commemorative items, particularly in earthenware and stoneware which appealed to the masses. Porcelain was employed for this purpose on comparatively few occasions, possibly because it was deemed too fine and expensive a material for popular taste. Among the subjects celebrated in the wares of eighteenth-century potters were the capture of Portobello by Admiral Edward Vernon in 1739, the protracted struggle of John Wilkes against the political Establishment of the 1760s, the French Revolution (1789–92) and the secession of the thirteen North American colonies (1776–83). It is surprising, but true, that a great amount—perhaps even the major portion—of the bowls, plates and dishes celebrating General George Washington and the American victories on land and sea were manufactured in the Staffordshire potteries. Josiah Wedgwood even produced an excellent stoneware version of the Rattlesnake emblem which, with the motto 'Who dares tread on me', formed one of the early flags of the United Colonies during their struggle for independence. Political and imperial sentiments were subordinated in the never-ending quest for rich markets, though I cannot imagine that any present-day English manufacturers catering to the export trade would 'back Britain' in such an apparently anti-British fashion!

Apart from commemorating specific persons and events, the eighteenth-century potters and silversmiths manufactured items which had a certain central theme. The invention of the hot-air balloon by the Montgolfier Brothers in 1783 and the subsequent ascents by Pilatre de Rozier and Vincent Lunardi sparked off a craze for ballooning, or 'aerostation' as it was once known: this in turn led to the production of a wide variety of objects, from porcelain and pottery to fan leaves and watch cases, decorated with balloons, ascending, descending or simply drifting across the countryside. Where a specific balloon flight can be identified (if not by the inscription, by the background or on stylistic grounds) the value of such items can be double or treble that of an object which does not allude to a specific occasion.

The early nineteenth century also produced its crop of commemorative occasions. The most fertile of these were probably the Battles of Trafalgar and Waterloo, which resulted in a veritable rash of commemorative items, from engraved glass goblets to earthenware dishes, from elaborately chased silver vinaigrettes and snuff boxes to decorated hand carts. Collectors of Trafalgar material are interested in a cross-section of all the artistic media of the time: prints, books, pottery, glass, silver, medals, fan leaves— even furniture with pictorial marquetry embellishment. Each item, taken in isolation, has a certain value simply because of its subject interest; but a collection of items linked by the common denominator of the subject commemorated would be worth a handsome premium over the aggregate of the values of the individual pieces.

The examples quoted above are all outside the period covered by this book, and are in the true category of antiques. In one sense they all differ from the majority of the commemorative items which do come into the non-antique period in so far as they were never deliberately manufactured on a wide scale either before or just after the event commemorated. Although a few items were produced for the coronations of George III, George IV and William IV, the first occasion on which objects were manufactured in anticipation of an event on a grand scale, cashing in on its topicality, was the Coronation of Queen Victoria in 1838. Apart from the medals struck at the time there were plates, vases and ornaments which alluded in their inscriptions or decoration to the event being celebrated. Once the Coronation had taken place, the production of these souvenirs ceased—unlike the items which marked the opening of Sunderland Bridge in 1796 and were produced continuously for some thirty years afterwards.

The souvenirs which greeted the Coronation of the young queen were as nothing to those produced in celebration of her Golden Jubilee in 1887 and her Diamond Jubilee in 1897. Incidentally, new series of postage stamps and coins appeared at the time of the Golden Jubilee, though these were not commemorative in the strict sense. There was, however, a plethora of commemorative medallions, plaques, dishes, mugs, vases, boxes, paperweights and trivia of all kinds, the successful marketing of which certainly stimulated the souvenir industry to surpass itself ten years later. From then onwards, Royal Occasions in Britain provided splendid opportunities for the souvenir manufacturers, although it is only in comparatively recent times that a conscious attempt has been made to produce objects of great aesthetic beauty and superlative craftsmanship worthy of the occasion.

The vast majority of souvenirs produced for special events have had little intrinsic value. In this class belong the countless thousands of earthenware mugs presented to schoolchildren all over the country in celebration of the various Coronations. Doultons manufactured some 60,000 mugs for presentation to schoolchildren in commemoration of the Golden Jubilee of Queen Victoria, and the examples which have survived the ravages of the past eighty years are highly prized. But many lesser potteries also produced their quota of Jubilee mugs and, although often of inferior workmanship, they are eagerly sought after on account of their connection with this event.

The Coronations of King Edward VII in 1902 and King George V in 1911 were lavishly commemorated in mugs. A very large collection connected with either Coronation can be formed, since many School Boards, Corporations and civic bodies had their own distinctive designs. Similar presentations of mugs were made to mark the Silver Jubilee of King George V in 1935 and the Coronation of King George VI in 1937. Other souvenirs of these events, now eagerly sought after, range from cut-glass bowls with commemorative inscriptions to the silver cups presented to the babies born on Coronation Day 1937.

Apart from the mugs presented to children, there were vast quantities of other items produced for general sale to the public as souvenirs of these occasions. Plaques and plates, vases and figures, prints, posters and postcards and even bottles of specially brewed beer—all are now in great demand. The souvenir industry has to begin production many months before the event itself takes place, and one of the hazards, which the manufacturers insure against, is the likelihood of the event being cancelled or postponed. Thus, in 1937, a large amount of souvenirs had to be destroyed on account of the abdication of King Edward VIII the previous December. The comparatively few souvenirs of his Coronation, which never took place, are of particular interest to collectors, partly because of the popularity of the Duke of Windsor engendered when he was Prince of Wales and partly because of that perversity of collectors who are attracted to a 'non-event' more than to an actual happening. Consequently, Edward VIII souvenirs (like the few coins minted in certain parts of the Commonwealth during his brief reign) possess an appeal which far outweighs their intrinsic worth and fetch high prices when they come on the market.

Souvenirs commemorating the marriage of Princess Elizabeth and the Duke of Edinburgh in 1947, and the Silver Wedding of King George VI and Queen Elizabeth the following year, were produced on a comparatively limited scale, since wartime austerity was still making itself felt. These events do not seem to have captured the interest of collectors to the same extent as Coronations, and consequently, although the supply of material is short, the demand is correspondingly small. The Coronation of Queen Elizabeth in 1953, however, with all its connotations of the dawn of a new Elizabethan era and the hopes which that inspired, was extremely popular with the souvenir hunters, and the range of collectable objects produced was far greater than ever before. For the first time the top-quality manufacturers began producing special limited editions of souvenirs—the Queen's Beasts by Doultons are good examples. Stevens & Williams of Royal Brierley Crystal produced a glass loving cup inscribed with the royal coat of arms, Her Majesty's words of dedication of service and symbols of the Commonwealth countries. Only fifty of these loving cups were produced, and they were eagerly snapped up. Among the many other kinds of Coronation glassware, usually engraved with the royal cypher and the date, were vases, powder bowls, ash trays, wine glasses, butter dishes and cocktail shakers. In the commemorative glassware of the past twenty years there has been a distinct break with the hackneyed traditions of the Victorian and Edwardian eras. The glassware which commemorated the Coronation of Queen Elizabeth, in particular, was consciously designed to be in harmony with modern times, while the craftsman himself showed a new vitality and creative feeling. Traditional forms and styles have not been without influence, but in the majority of cases they have been adapted to the modern idiom.

Events of a public rather than a royal nature which have inspired the production of the better-quality souvenirs in recent years have included the British Empire Exhibition (1924–5), the Festival of Britain (1951), the quatercentenary of William Shakespeare (1964) and the death of Sir Winston Churchill (1965). Quite a sizeable collection of items related to each of these events could be made: mugs, plaques, medals, glassware, figures, silk pictures and crested caddy spoons being but a few of the disparate objects produced in their connection.

The most important recent event from the collector's viewpoint was the Investiture of the Prince of Wales at Caernarvon in July 1969. This inspired a wide range of souvenirs—good, bad and indifferent—on a grander scale, perhaps, than those produced for the Coronation of 1953. It is unfortunate that so much of the material produced in connection with the Investiture was tawdry and unworthy of the event. The Council of Industrial Design condemned in no uncertain terms the cheap-jack souvenirs—badly designed and poorly executed—and endeavoured to promote a higher standard by offering prizes for excellent designs. It is significant that those prizes were subsequently won by companies whose names have been in the forefront of their respective industries for hundreds of years. The popularity of the Prince and the vast amount of publicity which preceded the Investiture both combined to spark off a collecting mania for this event on an unprecedented scale. This is understandable, bearing in mind the higher standards of affluence generally and an uncertainty about

178

the future of money prevailing in Britain today, compared with sixteen years ago, when people did not have the same amount of money to spend on Coronation souvenirs.

Although medals are outside the scope of this book, I should mention the fact that, although the boom in commemorative medals received a severe setback following the British Government's clamp-down on gold medals in 1966, this facet of the souvenir industry has regained its former momentum, and as a result there was a flood of Prince of Wales medals in 1969. To mention but one manufacturer, John Pinches Limited produced several interesting and attractive medals. One design has the Prince's profile on the obverse and three ostrich plumes on the reverse. It was produced in two sizes ($1\frac{3}{4}$-inch and $1\frac{3}{8}$-inch diameters) which were sold as a set, in Britannia standard silver with a highly polished proof finish, encased in plush-lined boxes. They were numbered consecutively and only 1000 were available in silver at £13 13s 4d a set. Naturally these medals were not manufactured in gold, but the Government ban does not apply to platinum, so a very limited edition (twenty-five sets) was produced in this costly metal at £615 ($1,464) a set. Another design, showing the Prince on the obverse and Caernarvon Castle on the reverse, was produced in Britannia silver in three sizes and in varying quantities (though sets of the three, priced at £30 15s ($73), were limited to an edition of 500). A series of medallions of coin size was also produced; the four medals approximated to the shilling, florin, half-crown and crown denominations and sold as a set for about £22 ($53). On account of their small size and high intrinsic value these commemorative medals are extremely popular and have probably a more widely based appeal than any other souvenir produced in celebration of the Investiture.

In the ceramic line three companies in the Wedgwood Group produced interesting and attractive mementoes of the occasion. Josiah Wedgwood & Sons Ltd manufactured an elegant Queen's Ware mug, designed by Professor Richard Guyatt, showing crowns and the insignia of the Prince of Wales in gold and black, with the inscription GOD BLESS THE PRINCE OF WALES in English and Welsh. Another Queen's Ware mug was designed by Carl Toms and reproduced an early nineteenth-century print of Caernarvon Castle. Norman Wilson, formerly Wedgwood's production director, designed an attractive mug in black basalt. The insignia and inscriptions were done in gold. Three hexagonal money-boxes in traditional Wedgwood materials were also produced. Robert Minkin designed these boxes in black basalt, sage green and white jasper, and Queen's Ware respectively. Wedgwood's subsidiary

179

company, Coalport China Ltd, produced two versions of a fine bone china goblet designed by Donald Brindley. An unlimited edition of the gold design on white was made at £7 8s ($18), but only 500 were manufactured in gold on cobalt blue, retailing at £15 17s 6d ($38). A certificate signed by the chairman of Coalport, Mr E.W. Brain, accompanied each of the cobalt blue goblets. The gold decoration showed the façade of Caernarvon Castle and heraldic pennants, with the inscription of 'Charles, Prince of Wales, presented to the people by Her Majesty the Queen at Caernarvon Castle on 1st July 1969'. For William Adams & Sons Ltd, Robert Minkin designed a low-priced, half-pint mug which was released in an unlimited edition and made of Micratex, a specially strengthened earthenware. Although future antiquarian interest in these souvenirs must, to some extent, be linked to the initial retail price as well as the size of the edition, the Adams mug at 6s 9d (81¢) is as collectable an item as the Coalport goblet. Indeed, it is often the cheap, mass produced item which has a nasty habit of becoming comparatively rare, since few people bothered to collect it while it was currently available or bothered to look after it properly. If you are collecting the objects connected with one particular event they all possess the same basic desirability, even if some are rarer or more valuable than others.

In glassware, souvenirs of the occasion were produced by Whitefriars and Royal Brierley. The former consisted of a goblet beautifully engraved with the emblems of the Prince of Wales and issued in a limited edition of 500 at 30 guineas ($74).

Royal Brierley's goblet was hand copper-wheel engraved with a design by Tom Jones showing the Prince of Wales's feathers and the inscription DUW FENDITHIO DYWYSOG CYMRU (God bless the Prince of Wales). This was produced in a limited edition and retailed at £12 10s ($29). Tom Jones also designed a mug decorated with bright acid etching and retailing at £4 10s ($10). The design incorporated the three feathers, the leek and daffodil and the Welsh dragon, with the inscription INVESTITURE CAERNARVON CASTLE 1ST JULY 1969 round the rim.

ASSOCIATION ITEMS

At an auction held in Measham in February 1969 the following items fetched these remarkable sums: a battered brown enamelled mug, £17 ($41); four pairs of well-worn socks, £5 ($12); a canvas shoe, £11 ($26). Why was it that such ordinary, mundane articles should excite such keen bidding and fetch ridiculously high prices? The answer lies in their association with the Great Train Robbery which took place near Linslade in Buckinghamshire in August 1963. The daring with which this crime was committed and the vast amount of money stolen fired the public's imagination. It is unfortunate that crimes of this enormity are seen in a somewhat romantic light by many people. From Robin Hood and Ned Kelly to Bonnie and Clyde, thugs and robbers have been glorified. The sensational trials of the Great Train Robbers and the heavy sentences of imprisonment meted out to them seem only to have accelerated the process of glorification, and these criminals have indeed become a living legend. Books and countless articles have been written about them, and at least one film has been made. It is small wonder therefore that the interest of the public should turn to the material things linked with the Robbers. It is some consolation, if only a small one, to know that the fantastic sum realized by the sale of the Robbers' effects has helped to offset the £2 million ($4.8m) never recovered since the robbery took place.

Each lot in this particular sale was accompanied by a certificate attesting its provenance. It cannot be over-emphazised that provenance is the most important factor in establishing the significance and value of association items, since without it the object has nothing to distinguish it from any other similar item. I remember once seeing in someone's glass cabinet a wine-glass with a smudge of lipstick on the rim. This was proudly pointed out as having been used by a certain member of the Royal Family at some function or other at which the owner of the cabinet happened to be present and managed to purloin the glass after the meal as a souvenir. I am not sure whether the Royal fingerprints have been preserved on the bowl or stem of this glass; and as far as I am aware, lip-prints are not so distinctive. There is therefore little or nothing on this glass to prove its royal connection, and its value to a collector of items associated with this royal personage is doubtful. At best it can only serve as a memento of a pleasant and august occasion, and such value as it has must be personal to the proud possessor.

To establish the provenance of an item is usually very difficult, and the difficulty increases the farther back in time one goes. It is very seldom, for example, that a piece of jewelry can be attested by the existence of a contemporary painting showing the lady wearing the item in question. The antiquity of a tradition relating to items associated with a historical personage is no guarantee either. An interesting case is provided by the hat and pair of shoes known as King Henry's Tokens for the Manor of Ayot St Lawrence. The story goes that Nicholas Bristowe was riding with the King and Anne Boleyn in Hertfordshire and, passing Ayot St Lawrence, he

181

greatly admired the place, wondering whose it was. The King said, 'It is mine, but now shall be yours.' When Bristowe asked what evidence he was to produce of the gift, the King gave him the hat he was wearing and asked the Queen for her slippers, saying, 'Bring me these in London and I will give you the title deeds.' The hat and slippers have since always gone with the Estate. The story is obviously apocryphal, for Ayot St Lawrence was not forfeit to the Crown until after Anne Boleyn's death, and was obtained in the 'normal' manner by Bristowe (The Clerk of the Jewel House) in 1543.

Yet experts agree that the hat and shoes are mid-seventeenth century in style and appearance and must have been made at least a hundred years after the event with which they are supposed to be linked. Nevertheless, they made £270 ($648) when sold at Christie's in March 1969. Their undoubted antiquity, and the rarity of the hat in particular, assured them a ready sale, but it can only be conjectured how far the tale of King Henry VIII affected the price realized.

Coming nearer our own time, however, items connected with the past are not only more plentiful, but it is rather easier to verify their association. This is particularly true of clothing, where it is possible to check the item against photographs and paintings more easily than with antique items. The initials or name of the owner, or those of the dressmaker, may also assist identification. Underclothing, for obvious reasons, is much more difficult to authenticate and may be virtually impossible unless there is some identifying mark. Not so long ago, for example, a gentleman was interviewed on a BBC radio programme: he claimed to own a pair of stockings worn by Queen Victoria which he intended to sell for £100 ($240) or near offer. When questioned on the provenance of the stockings, he merely stated that they had come from an unimpeachable source. No attempt was made to prove their authenticity from their size or markings, yet other stockings, known to have belonged to the Queen, are recorded with the VR monogram and a serial number. Incidentally, one lot at Christie's costume sale in March 1969 contained several pairs of stockings, a chemise, a shawl and a nightgown, all reputedly the personal property of Queen Victoria.

Documentary evidence is extremely useful in establishing the provenance of an object connected to some famous person or event. This may take the form of a letter, or a bill of sale, referring to the object, and written by or to the person concerned. It happens occasionally that an object has been disposed of by auction and the celebrity in question has either bought or sold it. The auction catalogue and the printed list of prices realized (which often give the names of purchasers as well as the sums paid) serve as useful ancillary documentation. Thus it becomes an easy matter to trace the pedigree of an object, often of great intrinsic or antiquarian value in itself, if it has had a succession of famous owners. At the sale of the late Somerset Maugham's effects a sixteenth-century Spanish table made £4000 ($9600). As a fine example of its kind it was worth, perhaps, half that sum at most—but because it happened to be the table at which the celebrated novelist sat and wrote some of his best known works its value soared enormously. Admittedly emotional factors also governed the price realized by this table, for it was eventually knocked down, after intensely fierce bidding, to another writer, Godfrey Winn, who had been a close friend and admirer of Maugham. It is interesting to speculate what this table will fetch, if and when it again comes into the sale room. Much will depend on the literary standing of both Somerset Maugham and Godfrey Winn at that time and whether the same personal desire to possess this table at all costs enters into the spirit of the bidding.

The value of association items may vary considerably—and alarmingly—from one decade to the next, and from one country to the next, depending largely on the topicality or popularity of the person with which they are connected. After the Second World War the personal effects of the late, unlamented Nazi leaders— Hitler, Goering, Goebbels and the rest—were disposed of in a series of sales. The prices paid were ridiculously small—barely sufficient to cover the expense of the sales. Today, however, there is a curious, sick, interest in Nazi relics, and anything personally associated with the arch-criminals themselves commands big money. Anyone sensible (or perhaps I should say cynical) enough to have invested in these relics twenty years ago would have done very well out of it in view of the staggering world-wide demand for Nazi mementoes.

Since association can add greatly to the value of an item, it follows that the value will be greatest in a country where the person associated with the object is especially venerated and, conversely, almost worthless in a part of the world where the person is unknown. I came across a curious example of this quite recently. The Fitzgerald Collection of airmail stamps and souvenirs at the British Museum contains, among many other things, an envelope bearing a stamp used by the Russian consulate in Berlin in 1922 to frank mail carried by a private air service to Moscow. Since this service was of short duration and limited to official correspondence, these Russian consular air stamps are very elusive and particularly scarce on cover. The cover in the Fitzgerald Collection bears the earliest date known—a fortnight earlier than that hitherto regarded as the first date of use—and for this reason it is a most desirable item for the airmail specialist, with a value of, perhaps, £100 ($240). The envelope, however, was addressed to Bela Kun, the leader of the short-lived Hungarian Red Republic, who had fled to Moscow when his Communist regime was crushed in June 1919. In the early 1920s he was employed in Moscow by the Comintern to supervize subversive activities in Germany, and it is to be supposed that the letter which this envelope contained dealt with some matter of this nature. To an airmail collector this envelope is interesting philatelically, but no more. To the Hungarian People's Republic, on the other hand, it was considered to be such a desirable gem that the authorities in Budapest flew me out to Hungary in order to have the envelope displayed in a place of honour in the exhibition marking the golden jubilee of the Red Republic. The amount of interest generated by this unprepossessing item was quite staggering, including press, radio and television coverage. After the collapse of his regime, Bela Kun had been interned for a brief time in Austria, and the ration card, which had been issued to him during his internment, has survived in private hands in that country. Unfortunately the Hungarians were unable to persuade the owner of this document to lend it for their exhibition. To most people such a ration card would only be of passing interest, but to the Hungarians it would be of enormous value.

11 Coins

Next to philately, numismatics—the study of coins and medals—
is the largest of the acquisitive hobbies, in terms of number of
collectors, clubs, literature and organized trading. It still lags
behind stamp collecting as a popular pursuit, but the interest in
coins has been so phenomenal in recent years that numismatics
has made enormous strides, and if the present growth rate is
maintained it should catch up with philately in the 1970s. Ten
years ago there were fewer than thirty coin collectors' clubs in
Britain and even fewer coin dealers. Periodicals devoted to the
subject were non-existent, and numismatics received little or no
attention in the national press. Today there are well over 100
collectors' clubs and societies, almost 200 full-time coin dealers and
many part-timers and a Professional Numismatists' Association
has been established. In 1964 Link House Publications produced
Coins and Medals as a quarterly. Two years later the format was
enlarged and the magazine increased in frequency to a monthly.
Shortly afterwards a rival publication, *Coin Monthly*, appeared on
the scene and in 1967 a weekly newspaper (with coloured illustrations) entitled *Coins Medals and Currency*. Both *Coins and Medals* and
Coin Monthly produce excellent year books, containing useful
reference material. In the United States, where coin collecting
has always been more popularly based than in Britain, the periodi-
cal literature on the subject is much more prolific, and wider
attention is given to numismatics in the lay press.

Coins, with a history stretching back twenty-seven centuries, are
among the oldest antiques one could imagine. The indestructi-
bility of gold and silver, in which metals many coins were struck,
has meant that even the earliest coins of Asia Minor and Greece
have survived in surprisingly good condition. For £20–£30
($48–$72) one can, even now, purchase an Athenian tetradrachm
minted in the time of Pericles, and there are countless other silver
coins two thousand years old which can still be bought for even

smaller sums. The law of supply and demand operates in numismatics as in everything else. While the demand for the classical issues of Greece and Rome and the medieval hammered coinage of Europe is relatively small, there is always the problem of the supply being affected by the discovery of coin hoards. Overnight a coin hitherto regarded as excessively rare may become relatively common as a result of a hoard of similar pieces coming to light. The bulldozers and mechanical diggers of builders and property developers have brought to the surface a fantastic amount of fine numismatic material in recent years—the Serooskerke hoard in the Netherlands and the Newstead Abbey hoard in England being but two of the major finds which have had a dramatic impact on the market in classical and medieval coins.

Antique coins are of absorbing interest to the scholar, the classicist and the historian, but as an investment they are problematical. Unless they exist in sufficient quantities already and have a large following—so that the discovery of an important hoard is unlikely to affect their market value—they are best left alone. Comparatively modern coins in fine condition are becoming increasingly difficult to find. They have long held the interest of numismatists, and the large influx of new collectors in recent years has virtually dried up the supply, with the inevitable spiralling of prices.

The practice of collecting the coins of one country in depth— the study of mint marks, die variations and, above all, the different dates found on each denomination—originated in the United States. These collectors were isolated to a large extent from the sources of classical and medieval material in Europe, and therefore turned their attentions to the coinage of their own country. Apart from the very rare colonial coins produced before the American Revolutionary War of 1776–83 the coinage of the United States may be said to commence with the first Flying Eagle cents of 1792–3. The entire range of American coinage is therefore comparatively modern. The early coins are now moving into the expensive category, so collectors have tended to confine their interests to the coins issued since 1859, when the first of the Indian Head cents made their appearance. American collectors for many years have followed the practice of collecting each denomination in series, each date, mint mark and prominent die variation being included. This form of collecting has been stimulated by the publication of pocket-sized check-lists, showing which dates are the elusive ones, and by the production of coin wallets and folders designed to hold the complete range of dates for each denomination from the Indian Head and Lincoln cents to the silver dollars.

186

This form of collecting has gradually spread to other parts of the world during the past decade. In the past five years alone there has been something of a revolution in British numismatics. From being the dignified, rather academic pursuit of a select few, it has developed into a popular hobby of countless millions; everyone, from schoolboys to tycoons, from housewives to manual workers, is apparently checking through his or her small change in search of the scarce dates. Apart from the magazines mentioned above, there are numerous handbooks and catalogues, and at least half a dozen pocket guides to the British coins likely to be encountered, with indications of their mintage and value in various grades of condition.

Impending decimalization has given further impetus to coin collecting in Britain. The appearance of the first decimal coins in circulation and the release of specimen sets are arousing more interest at the moment than any other single factor. The great amount of well-timed publicity attending the gradual changeover to decimal coins has made the public far more aware of the obsolescence of the halfpenny and the halfcrown than of the humble farthing ten years ago. Brilliant uncirculated specimens from the last year of minting (1956) now retail at anything from 15s to £1 ($2.40), and many of the people who were caught napping by the demise of this coin have been wondering whether the same thing would happen to the halfpenny.

Speculation in sealed £5 bags of newly minted halfpennies reached ridiculous lengths in 1967 after it was announced that no coins of this denomination would be minted after 1967. At one point dealers were offering these bags at anything up to £11 ($26) as 'an investment', and presumably were finding ready customers at that inflated price. Then a spokesman for the Royal Mint stated that, so long as there was a demand for halfpennies, they would continue to be minted. This demand has turned out to be almost entirely from collectors and dealers, and the Mint has obligingly continued to produce these coins at a cost more than double their face value. Collectors have paid as much as a shilling each for these halfpennies, in the belief that impending demonetization would enhance their value considerably. A look at the mintage figures, however, indicates that whatever other halfpennies will go up in value, there should be no shortage of those dated 1967. With the exception of 1961, halfpennies have been minted in every year of the present reign until 1967. The numbers produced have fluctuated considerably, from under 9 millions in 1953, to 97 millions in 1965. During 1967 no fewer than 89 million halfpennies were minted and, since minting was continuing during 1968, the total number of 1967 halfpennies was in excess of 100 millions—a record for this denomination. When it is remembered that only two million farthings were minted in 1956, it will be realized that the chances of the 1967 halfpenny ever becoming a comparable rarity are very small. Nevertheless, the belief that halfpennies—of any date and condition—will become worthwhile collector's pieces seems to persist.

The halfcrown was destined for a slightly longer life, but already speculation in this denomination has been rife. The retail prices, at the time of writing, for brilliant uncirculated specimens range from £8 ($19) for 1954 coins to 6s (72¢) for 1967 coins. On the basis of numbers minted it is difficult to understand why 1954 should be considered such a good year; a mintage of 11,500,000 compares very favourably with 1959 (9 millions), 1964 (just under 6 millions) or 1965 (6,500,000), but bearing in mind the degrees of numismatic interest aroused since 1964, it is to be presumed that a larger quantity of halfcrowns of that and subsequent dates have been laid aside in uncirculated condition. Conversely, the relatively scarce 1953 halfcrown (3,883,214 minted) in uncirculated condition rates slightly less than the 1954 coin. In this case the bulk of the coins issued were released to the public in the special plastic cases as souvenirs of Coronation year, and thus a higher proportion than normal was preserved in uncirculated condition. Incidentally, American dealers, who until recently retailed these sets at about £3 10s ($8.40), have been buying them in at about £6 ($14.40) and breaking them up to get at the uncirculated coins, which are worth more than £12 as individual items. The dearth of cased sets, as a consequence of this action, has pushed their value in Britain up to £10 ($24) or more, and it seems likely that they will be a good investment in the long run.

Interest in halfcrowns is by no means confined to those of the present reign, and several startling discoveries have been made recently in the earlier series. For Mr Horace Burrows of Chelmsford, Essex, the habit of checking his change automatically for elusive dates paid off handsomely when he discovered a halfcrown bearing the date 1952, hitherto unrecorded. A great amount of publicity was given to this find, much of it of a sensational nature, but no other specimens have come to light, so it must be supposed that, for once, that grossly overworked adjective 'unique' really applies. This coin bore the marks of extensive circulation, yet of all the countless thousands of people who must have handled it during its fifteen years in circulation, only Mr Burrows was observant and knowledgeable enough to profit by it. He has since disposed of it to an American collector for a sum reputedly in excess of £2000 ($4800).

The advent of decimalization will mean the disappearance of all the other denominations now current, except the shilling and the florin. Consequently, numismatic activity in the obsolescent denominations is very brisk at the moment and, indeed, certain dates of some coins have virtually disappeared from circulation. Bearing in mind, however, that modern British coins are usually produced in editions running into millions, it would require a very great demand from collectors to affect the incidence of a coin in circulation. Notable exceptions are some of the earlier brass threepennies: those dated 1946 and 1949, for example, released in editions of 620,000 and 464,000 respectively, are very seldom seen in circulation, and even fairly worn specimens would be worth a handsome premium over face value should they turn up in change. In uncirculated condition, however, they are so rare that they currently command about £14 ($33) and £30 ($72) respectively and approximately half these sums in extremely fine condition.

The numismatic market in sixpences fluctuated wildly during the year 1968–1969, since many people, with the same idea, hastened to acquire as many of these little coins as possible before they became obsolete. The true value of uncirculated modern sixpences is hard to assess, on account of the fact that comparatively large quantities of this denomination have survived in uncirculated condition. The retail price of 1942 sixpences (hitherto a relatively scarce date) slumped when a large quantity in sealed mint bags was suddenly released. An uncirculated 1942 sixpence is today worth about 15s—compared with 25s for a 1946 sixpence, though the value of the latter may be affected by the recent auction of 1500 of this date. At the time of writing these coins have not yet been dispersed into the retail market, and it is difficult to say whether a comparative drop in the ocean of 43½ millions minted will make any difference to the price. The rarest sixpence of modern times is that dated 1952, of which little more than a million were minted. Today, an example of this coin found in change would be worth at least 5s (60¢) and probably more if it were not too worn. In uncirculated condition it currently retails for about £10 ($24). The most expensive Elizabethan sixpences are those dated 1954 and 1955, which retail at 25s ($3) in uncirculated condition, although well over 100 millions of each date were minted. The startling difference between an ordinary, worn sixpence of these dates and uncirculated specimens only serves to emphasize the paramount importance of the condition factor in numismatic values. The sixpence, so useful in telephone boxes and parking meters, suffers so much more wear and tear in normal use than most other denominations that relatively few are to be found circulating in numismatically fine condition.

With the exception of 1953, when only 1,308,400 were issued, the Elizabethan penny is reasonably plentiful in the better grades of condition. During the year 1968–1969 the price for uncirculated 1953 pennies rose dramatically, from £1 to about £4 10s, and even in fairly worn condition currently retails for about 10s ($1.20). The last of the George VI pennies, however, include some of the great *lacunae* of modern British coinage. In 1950, 240,000 were minted and only half that quantity in the following year, for circulation in certain colonies. Oddly enough more of the 1951 penny have survived in uncirculated condition, so that it is worth 25 per cent less than the 1950 coin in comparable state, though the poorer grades of 1951 penny are worth more than twice as much as the 1950 coin in similar condition.

One of the side-effects of devaluation was the increase in the scrap value of silver. In November 1967 the value of silver increased to 18s the ounce troy, which meant that, theoretically at least, coins minted before 1947, containing 0·500 silver, were now worth considerably more than their face value. Thus a 1946 halfcrown (30¢) suddenly became worth 3s 7d (42¢), and the smaller coins rose proportionately in value, from the sixpence (6¢) (9d) to the florin (24¢) (just under 3s). Silver coins minted before 1920, containing 92·5 per cent silver, increased in value accordingly. A halfcrown (30¢) of that period therefore became worth about 7s (84¢), with proportional increases in value for the lesser denominations.

This fact has accounted for the rapid disappearance of such silver coins as were still in circulation. A correspondent writing to *Coins and Medals* (August 1968 issue) gave details of the silver coins dating between 1916 and 1936 which had passed through his hands during 1966 and 1967, and noted that the number in 1967 was about half that for the previous year. The recall of silver by the banks can account for only a small proportion of the disappearing coins, and undoubtedly collectors and speculators are responsible for the sudden dearth of these pieces. This is borne out by the advertisements of dealers, 'investors' and others offering up to double face value for pre-1920 silver coins, regardless of their condition.

Concern over this situation was expressed in the annual report of the Royal Mint, in which it was hinted that steps would be taken to foil attempts by speculators to recover the scrap value of silver coins when they ceased to be legal tender during the next few years. Hitherto there had been nothing to hinder unauthorized persons from melting down British coins when they ceased to be legal tender. The first step to curb speculation was taken by the Board of Trade, which introduced an order in June 1968 imposing licence control to prevent the export of silver coins for melting down overseas. Under the terms of this order the export of silver alloy coins minted before 1947, other than coins exported in a quantity not exceeding ten, now requires an export licence.

Steps to extend the terms of the Gold and Silver (Export Control) Act of 1920 are also being taken. Under the present Act it is an offence to melt down gold or silver coins which are legal tender in the United Kingdom or any British possession or foreign country without a licence from the Treasury. The Government now propose to extend this control to cover demonetized bulk hoarding of silver coins, in much the same way as the Exchange Control (Gold Coins Exemption) Order of 1966 was introduced to stamp out gold coin hoarding and speculation in gold commemorative medals. It seems unlikely, however, that the recovery of the £25m. ($60m.) worth of silver still in circulation would justify the administrative costs involved in setting up and administering such a control. One suggestion, that the Mint should strike copper–nickel halfcrowns dated 1968, 1969 and 1970 and issue them only in exchange for pre-1947 silver coins, is hardly likely to be implemented.

The newcomer to numismatics—like the beginner in any of the acquisitive hobbies—is constantly advised against trying to tackle too wide a field. The arguments against general collecting are that one could never hope to attain completeness in such a collection and that it is better (and financially more sound) to have specialized knowledge of a narrow field than a smattering on a larger scale.

Against these time-worn arguments I feel that many of the collectors who have taken up numismatics in the past year or two are becoming frustrated by their inability to acquire certain key dates, mint marks or die variations which are exceptionally scarce. Moreover, the excitement of hunting through one's loose change for elusive dates eventually wears thin.

What is the answer, if the beginner (or even the medium collector) is not to lose interest? I would suggest making a collection of modern coins of the whole world, taking each new series as it is issued. Counteracting the disadvantage of having a non-specialized world-wide collection is the advantage of having cast the net as wide as possible, so that while some coins will show little or no appreciation as the years go by, others will make rapid progress.

191

No one in his right mind would consider forming a collection of all the postage stamps issued throughout the world, since the annual output is now somewhere in the region of 6000 items. Coins, on the other hand, are far less numerous, and the total output of new issues from April 1967 to April 1969 was about 250. All of these could be purchased at the time of issue for a sum not exceeding £120 ($288), or little more than £1 ($2.40) a week.

This figure does not, of course, take into account re-issues differing from previous coins only in date or mint mark. If one were to take every coin on a more specialized basis, accounting for differences in date and die, the financial outlay would be much greater, but not impossible—certainly no more than £5 ($12) a week.

It is a common practice in most countries to release special editions of coins, struck from specially polished dies either by hand or by machine at a slower rate than normal in order to produce coins of an exceptionally high quality.

Such special editions are known as proofs, and invariably they are produced in limited editions. Sometimes, where a coin is produced in cupro-nickel for normal circulation, proofs are struck in silver (for example, the Bhutanese sertums of 1966).

Numismatic dealers report that already many of the collectors who were introduced to the hobby by the craze for date-collecting have graduated to something of more lasting appeal and are turning their attention to coins of the whole world.

Several of the larger dealers in Britain and the United States operate excellent new-issue services by which a collector may be assured of getting a set of every issue as it is released. This is the most advantageous method of buying coins, since one buys new coins at their starting price and does not miss out on limited issues.

Another interesting trend in world new issues is the release of coins simultaneously in several countries for the same object. In October 1968 eleven countries released coins to mark the anniversary of the Food and Agricultural Organization. Among the issuing States were Bolivia, Burundi, Ceylon, Lebanon, Syria and Uganda, and in May 1969 special FAO coins were issued by China, Cyprus, India, Iraq, Jordan, Philippines, Turkey and the United Arab Republic. By the time the twenty-fifth anniversary comes round, in October 1970, it is expected that many more countries, particularly in the Afro-Asian bloc, will have released special coins for this purpose.

192

12 Postage stamps

The adhesive postage stamp first saw the light of day in May 1840. Thus, if we were to apply the 1830 date line, these tiny pieces of paper could not be considered as antiques. Applying the hundred-years' criterion, however, only the first thirty years of adhesive stamps can be classed as antiques. Although the practice of issuing stamps had extended to most of the civilized world by 1870, the number of different varieties which had been produced by that date barely exceeded 1000. Many of these are extremely rare, if not unique. In this category come the One Cent Black on Magenta of British Guiana, which last came on the market at a reputed $40,000 in 1940 and today is appraised for insurance at £200,000 ($480,000). Barely a dozen each of the Penny and Two-pence 'Post Office' Mauritius stamps exist today, and these now have a price tag of £18,000 (Gibbons) or $42,500 (Scott), putting them on a par with the most desirable Old Master paintings on a proportionate basis.

Conversely, there are a great many 'antique' stamps which are surprisingly cheap even now. Age alone is not a factor in determining the value of a postage stamp, and although the world market is vast, with the number of collectors currently estimated at 35–50 millions, certain stamps were issued in such astronomic quantities that there is no shortage of them even now. The British Penny Red, for example, was released in February 1841, and was in use for seventeen years before perforation was introduced. Perforated Penny Reds with stars in their upper corners were current from 1858 till 1864 when the stamps appeared with letters in all four corners and remained in use till 1880. Countless millions of Penny Reds were used during a period of forty years, and though certain rarities, such as the Penny Red of 1864 from Plate 77, are worth hundreds or thousands of pounds, the majority of these stamps must still be reckoned in pence or shillings.

Even the Penny Black, the world's first adhesive postage stamp,

N

though rising steadily in value, is still within the financial reach of most people.

Stanley Gibbons recount an anecdote concerning a lady who walked into their shop in the Strand one day claiming that she had a 'unique' Penny Black. When the shop assistant pointed out that their window contained an attractive display of fine copies, she exclaimed triumphantly, 'There you are—*yours* are only copies; mine is the *original*.'

Few people would be so naïve as to equate a postage stamp with a painting, a print or a drawing in this way, but it is surprising how the myth that the Penny Black is a rare stamp persists. The fact that in 1968 a single Penny Black fetched £1100 ($2600) in an auction and, more recently, a block on cover made £4800 ($11,500) would tend to reinforce this myth—until the facts are studied more closely.

Although the Penny Black was the very first stamp issued, 128 years ago, it is much commoner even now than many stamps issued since then. From the order books of Perkins Bacon who printed the stamps we know that 300,000 sheets were produced before January 1841, when it was superseded by the Penny Red.

Of the 72 million Penny Blacks printed it must be presumed that most, if not all, were actually put into circulation. Though this figure is admittedly smaller than that for any other British definitive stamp prepaying the inland letter rate, it compares favourably with many of the commemorative issues and is, incidentally, six times the size of the edition for the much-vaunted World Cup Winners stamp of 1966.

Of course, very few people took a philatelic interest in the Penny Black while it could be purchased at face value over the Post Office counter, and at least a decade elapsed before philatelic demand was born. On the other hand, it should be remembered that a century ago the receipt of a letter was such a rare occurrence for the average person that letters tended to be kept for years on end, instead of being tossed with their envelopes into the wastepaper basket.

During the lifetime of the Penny Black the new-fangled envelope had not caught on, and the normal practice was still to use the back of the letter itself as a wrapper; thus letter and wrapper seldom parted company. For this reason, therefore, there is a higher incidence in bundles of nineteenth-century correspondence of Penny Blacks and the early, imperforate Penny Reds than the later issues, which were discarded with the envelopes.

It would be difficult to estimate what proportion of these 72 million Penny Blacks has survived and, of that, what proportion is in really fine four-margined condition. The number of surviving Penny Blacks certainly runs into millions, but many of them have disappeared into collections of sheet reconstruction (2640 of them being required for a complete plating study), and good copies have never been easy to find.

Being produced without perforations, Penny Blacks had to be separated by scissors or knife, or were torn from the sheet with varying degrees of care. More often than not the stamps would be cut close on one or more sides, if not actually cut into. To produce a stamp with generous margins on all four sides would mean that four other stamps suffered as a consequence.

The Victorian fear that dishonest persons would attempt to remove the postmark and re-use the stamp resulted in very thorough obliteration of the stamps. Thus, lightly cancelled copies are at a premium.

Early collectors had a shocking disregard for the preservation of their specimens; having brutally removed a stamp from its letter, they would often thread it on to a stamp 'snake'—a popular Victorian pastime, judging by the number of pinholed Penny Blacks in existence.

The odds against a Penny Black surviving in four-margined, lightly cancelled condition, without thins, tears or pinholes are very great, and account for the price tag which the Gibbons' catalogue puts on the cheapest variety of used stamp. I say cheapest because philatelists distinguish between the eleven plates used (some recorded in more than one state) and prices vary from £6 ($14) for a stamp from Plate 5 to £45 ($108) for a specimen of Plate 11. Normally obliteration was effected by a black or red Maltese cross, but a yellow cross (used at Newnham on Severn) now rates £200 ($480).

Three other factors which greatly affect the value of the Penny Black are multiples, covers and dates used. A pair, for example, would be worth three times as much as a single, while the minimum price for a block of four jumps immediately to £100 ($240). The price for larger multiples increases even more sharply, since the number of large blocks in existence is comparatively small.

When the stamp is still adhering to its original cover or envelope the collector must expect to pay a premium, which may be quite considerable if the date of use is early.

The Gibbons' *Specialised Catalogue* prices covers used during the first month (May 1840) at a minimum of £12 ($28), though used on the very first day, 6 May, the price jumps to £120 ($288).

There is one cover which was used on the first day, and this, combined with the fact that a block of ten was used, makes it a highly desirable item. Harmer's put a price tag of £1500 to £2000 on it when it came up in their auction of 27 May 1968, but in fact it was knocked down at £4800 ($11,520).

Penny Blacks were on sale from 1 May onwards, but not valid till 6 May. A few were inadvertently used prematurely, and one of these, still attached to a small piece showing the Bath postmark of 2 May, was sold for £1100 ($2640) at Robson Lowe in March 1968 (more than double the auctioneer's estimate). The letters AA in the corners imply that it was probably the very first Penny Black ever used.

The postal services in the United States a century ago were less sophisticated than their European counterparts and, of course, the population of the country was only a fraction of what it is today. Since the number of stamp collectors in America today outnumbers the total population of the United States in 1850, it is almost inevitable that early American stamps should be relatively scarce and correspondingly more expensive than their British or European contemporaries. The first 5¢ (Washington) and 10¢ (Franklin) stamps of the United States were issued in 1847, and are catalogued today at £100 and £400 by Gibbons and at $175 and $700 respectively by Scott. Many of the local 'Postmasters' stamps of the 1840s which preceded the general issue of 1847 are major rarities, such as the Buchanan 5¢ (1845), the St Louis 'Bears' (1845–7) or the New Haven (1845). Even the low denominations of the 1869 pictorial series, current a century ago, are priced in pounds or dollars rather than in shillings or cents.

Somewhere midway between the extremes of British and American stamps of the very early period come the issues of the majority of European countries. Lower standards of living in the populations of these countries and lower standards of literacy generally militated against such a widespread use of the postal services as in Britain. In addition, Europe in the 1840s and 1850s was in a state of political transition, out of which emerged such powerful nation states as Germany and Italy. Consequently, the stamps of the numerous principalities and duchies, which disappeared at the unification of these countries, had a relatively brief usage, and many of them are scarce and expensive nowadays. The law of supply and demand also has an important effect on the value of many of these early stamps. Although there are more stamp collectors in America than in any other country, both Italy and Germany have a high density of stamp collectors in relation to the population in general, and these philatelists have stimulated the market in the early stamps of their respective countries.

196

Postage stamps had, by 1870, penetrated to all of the civilized countries and to a good number of the more backward ones as well, but communications on a global scale were severely limited till the twentieth century. By and large, the stamps issued by non-European countries more than a hundred years ago are likely to to be expensive today—providing that they are in good condition.

The stamps of the early period, from 1840 to 1870, are now regarded as the classics of philately. This was a period dominated by the beautiful line-engraved stamps of Perkins Bacon, a London firm which, in its heyday, produced the stamps for Britain, most of the British colonies and many other countries all over the world. In New York, Messrs Edson, Rawson, Wright and Hatch, later known as the American Bank Note Company, recess-printed the early issues not only of the United States but of Canada and many Latin American countries. The high standards of design and printing produced by these companies have contributed largely to the eternal appeal of the classic stamps, and though there are many other categories of stamps which have appeared since then, these are still the 'blue chips' of philately.

Contemporaneous with the fine line-engraved stamps produced in London and New York there were, in many of the more remote parts of the world, attempts to produce postage stamps from local resources. The so-called Primitives, naïve in design and mediocre (at best) in production, include some of the ugliest and crudest stamps ever foisted on the public. Yet they have a certain unsophisticated charm and a romantic background which has endeared them to collectors. This, coupled with the fact that most of them are extremely rare, has given them a popularity which far outweighs their aesthetic qualities, and the rarest of them exceed by a generous margin the rarest of the classics in market value. As well as the early issues of British Guiana and Mauritius already mentioned, the Primitives include such unlovely gems as the Hawaiian 'Missionaries' (1851), the 'Sydney Views' of New South Wales (1850), the Moldavian 'Bulls' (1858), the curious circular 'Tigers' of Afghanistan (1870), the 'Perot' stamps of Bermuda and many of the Postmaster issues of the United States. With the exception of the Afghan 'Tigers', the others are all in the four-figure ($2400 plus) bracket nowadays, and a few are worth considerably more.

After 1870 postage stamps, and philately (the science of stamp-collecting), entered a new phase. From then until the end of the nineteenth century postage stamps, in the main, ceased to be objects of beauty in themselves and became more functional in execution, though often more fussy in design. Over-elaboration in ornament was a common failing of stamps issued by Britain and the majority of countries in Europe and Latin America at this time. It was also the period when, in a bid to reduce production costs, the colonial powers (Britain, France, Germany, Portugal and Spain) used key-type designs uniformly throughout their overseas territories. The drab appearance of the stamps themselves did nothing to relieve the monotony of the key-type designs. The rather boring key-types coincided with a rush of provisional overprints and surcharges of a temporary nature, to which many countries were prone in the latter years of the nineteenth and early years of the twentieth centuries. These factors, which showed that most postal administrations were not interested in stamp collectors, led to a flagging of interest on the part of collectors themselves. After a brief flourishing of philatelic periodicals in the 1860s most of them died out in the ensuing decades. The world's oldest stamp magazines still in continuous publication are the *Philatelic Journal of Great Britain* (1891) and *The London Philatelist* (1892), and it is from that decade that philately in the modern, scientific sense really dates. Because the stamps of the 1870–1900 period often appear dull and uninteresting they have been neglected by collectors in the past. Yet to dismiss them lightly is a grievous mistake which is only now being rectified. A systematic study of the British surface-printed stamps in general, or even of the Penny Lilac of 1881–1901 in particular, yields a great deal of interest for the philatelist and not a little profit too, since the neglect of these stamps for more than seventy years means that there are many unconsidered trifles still waiting to be snapped up by the discerning collector, which will generously repay the original outlay. This period in philately, for so long in the doldrums, is now gaining an increasing amount of attention, and the market in these stamps is rapidly rising.

The pattern of colonial key-plates and rather monotonous designs elsewhere continued down to the time of the First World War and (particularly in the British and Portuguese colonies) survived into the 1920s. The war itself, however, produced a large crop of interesting issues of a provisional nature: overprints for use in the territories occupied by the Germans, from Belgium to Russian Poland and Roumania, British, Belgian and French overprints for use in the former German colonies, the stamps of the 'Successor States' which emerged out of the rubble of the Austro-Hungarian Empire, the issues of the Bolsheviks and the various factions which opposed them in Russia from 1917 onwards, the stamps of the plebiscite areas at the end of the war and, finally, the stamps of Poland, Finland and the Baltic States which broke

198

away from the Tsarist Empire at the time of the Russian Revolution. The stamps of that war and the immediate postwar years, however, must be treated with some caution. The British overprints for use in former German colonies rank among the rarest stamps of this century, and the occupation issues for Salonika (1916) and the Persian seaport of Bushire (1915) are decidedly scarce. But all too often it happened that soldiers invested in the stamps temporarily in use in the areas they were fighting over, and afterwards they tried to unload their speculative stock on to the philatelic market. While the war was still raging the craze for war stamps seemed limitless, but the boom ended abruptly in 1920. War-weariness, plus the imminence of economic depression, killed the interest in war stamps, and prices slumped disastrously overnight. It is only within the past fifteen years that these interesting stamps have made a comeback.

In 1959 the incomparable collection of First World War material formed by the late Marquess of Bute came under the hammer and realized a total of £59,048 ($141,715). Some of the stamps in this collection had suffered immersion in water when the London home of the Marquess was damaged in the Blitz, and, on the whole, the prices in this sale were not particularly outstanding. Nevertheless, the appearance of this collection in the sale room stimulated a great deal of attention to the stamps of the First World War, which, being by that time suitably remote in time, had begun to attract antiquarian interest. The Bute sale was the turning-point, and since then the prices of 1914–19 stamps and associated material have risen steadily—in some cases quite spectacularly. A case in point concerns the stamps used for a brief period (three weeks in May 1916) on a tiny island in the Gulf of Smyrna. The Royal Navy occupied the island of Makronisi (which translates into English as 'Long Island') in order to blockade the port of Smyrna. The Intelligence Officer attached to the expedition was appointed Civil Administrator of Long Island, and under his authority an issue of stamps was made. A few of these consisted of contemporary Turkish fiscal stamps overprinted by typewriter G.R.I. LONG ISLAND and surcharged in sterling, but the bulk of this curious issue was produced entirely by typewriting. On the whole, the stamps are remarkably free from errors in typing, but the use of various colours of carbon paper (black, blue or violet) added considerably to the number of different stamps produced. About thirty different stamps (Gibbons catalogue list twenty-eight of them) were produced altogether, and it would not be unreasonable to suppose that the perpetrator of this issue had a (conscious or unconscious) philatelic motive. The authenticity of

199

the stamps was questioned at the time of their appearance, and for many years they were under a cloud. The only catalogue to list them was Gibbons, and over a period of forty years they hardly moved upwards in price. This may, in part, have been due to the fact that they were very seldom seen on the market; in some cases fewer than a score of a particular stamp were produced and just how many of these have been preserved in the hands of collectors cannot be estimated. The prices paid for Long Island stamps in the Bute sale were reasonably good but not startling. Since then a few of these interesting items have come on the market and have excited an increasing amount of attention. At a Stanley Gibbons auction in 1968 a collection of Long Island stamps, estimated to fetch £300 ($720), went for exactly twice that sum.

Another overprinted British issue, made for use in an island where British forces were blockading the enemy, was also under a cloud for many years. The island of Mafia, off the East African coast, was occupied by British troops in 1915 in order to blockade the Rufiji Delta, in which the German warship *Königsberg* was hiding. The first issue of Mafia, consisting of German East Africa stamps overprinted G.R.I. MAFIA and surcharged in Indian currency, was long suspect, and it is only within very recent times that Gibbons have begun to list this series in the catalogue (although the German catalogue, *Michel Deutschland Spezialisiert Katalog*, has priced them for many years). As an issue made in a part of the erstwhile German colonies, the stamps of Mafia have long been popular in Germany, and the prices paid for them have been correspondingly high. On the other hand, they have been sadly neglected in Britain and, until now, such examples as came on the market were usually snapped up by Continental buyers for export to Germany, where they could be sold at a good profit. Today, however, the first issue of Mafia is properly recognized in Britain, and prices are keen on both sides of the North Sea.

The slump in the stamps of the First World War also dragged down the issues of 'Neurope', a term coined to denote the new countries, provisional administrations and plebiscite areas which had emerged from the holocaust. Philatelic revenue must have been a godsend to many of these countries, embarking on independence with an empty exchequer. While the craze lasted, vast quantities of stamps from Estonia, Latvia, Lithuania and the plebiscite territories of Allenstein, Memel and Schleswig poured on to the market. Every schoolboy collection of the 1920s contained a liberal sprinkling of these, and most of them have remained a drag on the market to this day. In passing, it should be noted that stamps produced in times of war and international upheaval are seldom a good investment in the long run. The troops returning to England after the Boer War unloaded large quantities of the wartime issues of the Orange Free State and the Transvaal, and the market in these stamps has been rather poor ever since. The Second World War had its crop of speculators—this time the British Military Administration stamps of Burma attracted their unwelcome attention, not to mention the 'Hitler Heads' of the Nazi regime. These stamps are—and probably always will be—a bad bargain.

The times of peace are not necessarily times of prosperity—a fact which has had some bearing on the investment potential of many stamps. In the 1920s and 1930s, for example, lengthy sets with a high face value were released by St Kitts-Nevis, St Helena, Montserrat, the Falkland Islands and Sierra Leone to commemorate their centenaries. Many British colonies around the same period issued ultra-high-value stamps in denominations of £5 and upwards. Unfortunately there were few collectors at the time who could afford to buy these stamps, since their appearance coincided with world economic depression and, as a result, relatively few of these long sets and ultra-high values were sold for philatelic purposes. These are the stamps which are now fetching comparatively large sums. Their value usually lies in hundreds of pounds rather than in thousands, and they are thus attractive to the British investor who does not wish to pay Capital Gains Tax on the profits on stamps which he may sell for more than £1000 ($2400). Stamps in the £200–£500 range are a better buy; if sold for less than £1000 each they do not attract Capital Gains Tax and should still yield a handsome profit over a reasonably short period. Below are listed some typical Georgian high values of the period between the wars, and also some of the famous 'long sets' which were issued about the same time. Their catalogue values in 1960 and 1969 are given for comparison, the 1969 Scott values in dollars.

	1960	1969	
Gibraltar £5	£38	£275	$325
Malta 10s 1919	£10	£300	$375
Cyprus £5	£50	£475	$900
Sierra Leone £5 1921	£48	£425	$425
Falkland Islands Centenary 1933 £1	£36	£150	$250
Montserrat Tercentenary 5s	£8	£25	$35
Sierra Leone Centenary £1	£30	£100	$200
St Helena Centenary 10s	£8	£30	$50
St Kitts-Nevis Tercentenary £1	£32	£225	$185

In the 1920s Kenya issued stamps in the very high denominations of £25, £50, £75 and £100. They were intended for fiscal purposes, but because they were inscribed POSTAGE & REVENUE they could theoretically be used postally, and were thus of interest to philatelists. For £250 ($600) one could have bought these over the post office counter forty years ago; today they are worth £32,000 ($76,800). The cents denominations of the same series could have been purchased, when current, for 2s 6d (30¢); today these low denominations are worth £3 ($7.20) in mint condition, an increase over face value of 2400 per cent.

Although philately is extremely popular in the United States, the stamps of that country do not lend themselves to investment to the extent that one might expect. In general, no stamps in the past fifty years have turned out to be worthwhile investments, with two notable exceptions. A set of three airmail stamps was issued in 1930 to mark the Atlantic flights of the *Graf Zeppelin* airship. This trio had a combined face value of $4.55 (worth just over £1 in sterling at the then rates of exchange). Today this set is priced by Scott at $575 and by Gibbons at £175. The release of the 'Zeppelins' when America was in the grip of the Depression meant that comparatively few of these handsome stamps were sold. Now that the United States is a prosperous country once more the demand for these stamps is great, and inevitably the price must soar as the demand increases. The other notable exceptions consist of the 10¢ denominations in the sets of Famous Americans issued in 1940. These stamps are still reasonably cheap compared with the Zeppelins, since they had a lower face value and were bought in larger quantities. Apart from these issues, most American commemorative stamps are in low denominations, usually conforming to the current inland letter rate (with an occasional higher denomination for air mail), and since it has long been fashionable for Americans to invest in new issues in complete sheets, a plentiful supply of these stamps seems assured for many years to come. No United States stamps since 1869 have been demonetized, and all since that date are still valid for postage, though one would be foolish to use stamps of more than fifty years ago in this way.

Among the earlier American stamps which must be singled out as good investment material are the long sets commemorating the Columbus quatercentenary (1893), the Omaha Exposition (1898) and the Louisiana Sesquicentennial (1904). Stamp collectors at the time were scandalized by these long and expensive sets and, largely as a result, the Society for the Suppression of Speculative Stamps was formed. Important sections of the philatelic trade, however, refused to join in boycotting these stamps and, even then, there were plenty of collectors who felt they had to get these sets in order to complete their collections. With the passage of time the Columbus and the other long sets of seventy years ago have become respectable and are now highly priced. The Columbus set, with a face value of $16.34 is now priced by Scott at $1075 and by Gibbons at £550.

The other long set of the nineties which is often quoted as an example of an unpopular issue turned respectable is the Greek series for the first modern Olympic Games in 1896. This had a face value of 19 drachmae (about £1, $2.40 at contemporary rates of exchange) and is now listed at £190 ($456) by Gibbons. This set is now extremely popular, and will never diminish in popularity so long as Olympic stamps are collected. Every Olympiad since the Brussels Games of 1920 has been marked by an issue of stamps by the host country and, in recent years, numerous stamps have been released by other countries as well—including some which do not take part in the actual Games. There is a very real danger that frivolous issues, such as Winter Olympic stamps from Burundi (in the very heart of equatorial Africa where snow is unknown) or the Persian Gulf sheikhdoms, will bring Olympic philately into disrepute.

By the early 1930s most countries were beginning to abandon the strictly utilitarian, rather monotonous designs with which they had been satisfied and were embarking on pictorial definitive series. At the same time the frequency of commemorative issues began to increase. Instead of having long sets once in ten years, there was now a tendency to have one or two short sets (two to four denominations) every year. This pattern of short, frequent sets has been continued ever since, but nowadays even the most insignificant country feels that it must produce at least half a dozen special issues a year. In the 1930s there was also a return to the more traditional recess-printing as a method of production, and the use of two-colour combinations led to some pleasing results.

As early as 1914 the Kingdom of Bavaria had produced a definitive series, portraying Prince Regent Luitpold, by the photogravure process. It is odd that this cheap but highly versatile process did not catch on quickly elsewhere. Isolated examples of photogravure stamps appeared in Egypt (1922), Syria (1925) and the Gold Coast (1928), but a further decade elapsed before this process was at all widely accepted. The definitive issues of the Seychelles and the Virgin Islands in 1938 showed the capabilities of photogravure, and the majority of British stamps from 1934 onwards have been printed by this process. Photogravure was extended to many of the British colonies in the 1950s, and in the ensuing decade multicolour photogravure became increasingly common. The trend towards more colourful stamps was world-wide, and was characteristic of the issues made by the emergent nations of Africa and Asia in the postwar years. The United Kingdom adopted multicolour photogravure in 1961, but the major Commonwealth countries, such as Australia, Canada, India and Pakistan, were slower in utilizing it, while Canada (with one or two exceptions printed by lithography) has continued to use recess-printing. The United States, France and several other major countries have also stuck to recess-printing, though the invention of the Giori press has made multicolour work possible in this process also. In general, therefore, the postage stamps pro-duced throughout the world in the past ten years have brightened up considerably. Not only are they technically more varied and colourful but the design of stamps is now recognized as a distinct branch of miniscule art. More interesting designs and more fre-quent issues (now averaging about 6000 annually) have stimu-lated the interest of collectors as never before and brought a vast number of new recruits to the hobby.

Philately today is the largest of the acquisitive hobbies, with ramifications in every part of the world. It is highly organized, from the Fédération Internationale de Philatelie (FIP) at the international level to the national unions and congresses, the county and provincial federations and the clubs and societies which meet regularly in every town of any size. In Britain there are about 400 philatelic societies affiliated to the British Philatelic Association (and many others which have not bothered to join). The number of collectors in these societies amounts to no more than 15,000—though it has been estimated that there are now between 2 and 3 million collectors in the United Kingdom. In the United States there are some 8000 clubs and perhaps 10 million collectors—about one in twenty of the population. Both Germany and Japan figure high in the list of countries with a high percen-tage of stamp-collectors, while Italy and France are also among the most philatelically conscious nations.

The turnover of the philatelic trade may seem small in com-parison with the fine arts and antiques as a whole. The three leading London auctioneers—Stanley Gibbons, H.R. Harmer and Robson Lowe—have a combined sale-room turnover of about £3m. ($7.2m.) a year, compared with ten times that sum from Sotheby's and Christie's alone. But it should be remembered that stamps represent only one, specialized facet of collecting, and the total sales of auctioneers, dealers, philatelic agencies and postal administrations must be a formidable sum. The British General Post Office has witnessed the gross sales from its Philatelic Bureau alone rise from £100,000 ($240,000) in 1964 to well over £3m. ($7.2m.) in 1969, and these figures do not take into account the philatelic sales at more than 25,000 post offices all over the country.

Stamps may be issued by the thousand or even by the million—and no other acquisitive hobby is concerned with such astronomical figures—but philately is all-pervasive, striking at all levels of society all over the world, and has an infinitely wider appeal than any of the other 'antiques of the future' discussed in this book. The market in stamps is truly international, and their comparatively small bulk has made them a favourite form of investment, particularly in times of political and economic upheaval. It is small wonder, therefore, that this 'hobby of kings, and king of hobbies' should be universally popular.

Bibliography

Victoriana
Amaya, M. *Art Nouveau* Studio Vista, London;
  E. P. Dutton, New York 1966
Buday, G. *The History of the Christmas Card*
  Spring Books, London 1964
Laver, J. *Victoriana* Ward Lock, London 1966
Mebane, J. *New Horizons in Collecting*
  Yoseloff, London 1967
Mebane, J. *The Coming Collecting Boom*
  Yoseloff, London 1968
Scott, A. and C. *Collecting* Joseph, London 1968
Staff, F. *The Valentine and its Origins*
  Lutterworth, London 1969

Silver
Curran, M. *Collecting English Silver* Arco,
  London 1963
Delieb, E. *Investing in Silver* Barrie &
  Rockliff, London 1967
Hughes, G. *Modern Silver Throughout the
  World 1880–1967* Studio Vista, London;
  Crown Publishers, New York 1967
Wardle, P. *Victorian Silver and Silver Plate*
  Jenkins, London 1963

Glass
Amaya, M. *Tiffany Glass* Studio Vista,
  London; Walker, New York 1967
Beard, G. *Modern Glass* Studio Vista, London;
  E. P. Dutton, New York 1968
Grover, R. & L. *Art Glass Nouveau* Prentice
  Hall, London; Tuttle, Tokyo 1967
Kämpfer, F. & Beyer, K. G. *Glass: A World
  History* Studio Vista, London; New York
  Graphic, Conn, 1966
Koch, R. *Louis C. Tiffany. Rebel in Glass*
  Crown Publishers, New York 1964
Savage, G. *Glass* Weidenfeld & Nicolson,
  London 1965

Glass paperweights
Cambell Cloak, E. *Glass Paperweights* Studio
  Vista, London; Crown Publishers, N.Y. 1969
Elville, E. M. *Paperweights and other Glass
  Curiosities* Country Life, London 1954

Porcelain
Dauterman, C. C. *Sèvres* Studio Vista,
  London; Walker, New York 1969
Fisher, S. *Worcester Porcelain* Ward Lock,
  London 1968
Godden, G. A. *Victorian Porcelain* Jenkins,
  London 1961
Lewis, G. *A Collector's History of English
  Pottery* Studio Vista, London; Viking Press
  New York 1969
Morley-Fletcher, H. *Investing in Pottery and
  Porcelain* Barrie & Rockliff, London 1968

Furniture
Bird, A. C. *Early Victorian Furniture* Hamilton,
  London 1964
Hayward, H. *World Furniture* Hamlyn,
  London 1965
Miller, E. G. *American Antique Furniture*
  Constable, London 1966
Moody, E. *Modern Furniture* Studio Vista,
  London; E. P. Dutton, New York 1966

Woven silk pictures
Baker, W. L. *The Silk Pictures of Thomas
  Stevens* Exposition Press, New York 1957
Darby, M. *Stevengraphs* published by the
  author 1969

The world in miniature
Fraser, A. *A History of Toys* Weidenfeld &
  Nicolson, London 1966
Fraser, A. *Dolls* Weidenfeld & Nicolson,
  London 1968
Hillier, M. *Dolls and Doll-makers* Weidenfeld
  & Nicolson, London 1968
Harris, H. *Model Soldiers* Weidenfeld &
  Nicolson, London 1962
Noble, J. *Dolls* Studio Vista, London;
  Walker, New York 1967
White, G. *European and American Dolls*
  Batsford, London 1966

Motor cars
Buckley, J. R. *Cars of the Connoisseur*
  Batsford, London 1960

Coins
Friedberg, R. *International Coin Catalogue and
  Price List* Coin and Currency Inst., New
  York
Mackay, J. A. *Value in Coins and Medals*
  Johnson, London 1968
Purvey, F. *Collecting Coins—For the Beginner*
  Foyle, London 1963
Seaby, P. J. (ed) *The Standard Catalogue of
  British Coins* Seaby, London 1968
Seaby, P. J. & Bussell, M. *British Copper Coins
  and their Values* Seaby, London 1968
Yeoman, R. S. *Catalog of Modern World Coins*
  Whitman, New York
Whitman *Handbook of United States Coins*
  Whitman, New York

Stamps
Garden, B. *Make Money with Stamps*
  Philatelic Publishers, London 1968
Mackay, J. A. *Money in Stamps* Johnson,
  London 1967
Narbeth, C. C. *Investing in Stamps*, Stanley
  Paul, London 1968

Index